PHILIP L. MARTIN

TRADE
AND MIGRATION

NAFTA
and Agriculture

Institute for International Economics
Washington, DC
October 1993

Philip L. Martin, Visiting Fellow, is Professor of Agricultural Economics at the University of California at Davis and a member of the Commission on Agricultural Workers established by the Immigration Reform and Control Act of 1986. He holds a Ph.D. in economics and agricultural economics from the University of Wisconsin and is the author of numerous studies and reports on immigration.

INSTITUTE FOR INTERNATIONAL ECONOMICS
11 Dupont Circle, NW
Washington, DC 20036-1207
(202) 328-9000 FAX: (202) 328-5432

C. Fred Bergsten, *Director*
Christine F. Lowry, *Director of Publications*

Printed in the United States of America
96 95 94 93   4 3 2 1

Library of Congress Cataloging-in-Publication Data

Martin, Philip L., 1949–
   Trade and Migration: NAFTA and Agriculture /Philip Martin.
      p.   cm.—(Policy analyses in international economics; 38)
      Includes bibliographical references and index.
   1. United States—Foreign economic relations—Mexico. 2. Mexico—Foreign economic relations—United States. 3. Free trade—United States. 4. Free trade—Mexico. 5. United States—Emigration and Immigration—Economic aspects. 6. Mexico—Emigration and immigration—Economic aspects. 7. Labor supply—United States. 8. Mexicans—Employment—United States. I. Title. II. Series.
   HF1456.5.M6M37   1993
   304.8'373072—dc20   93-2922
                                                  CIP

      ISBN 0-88132-201-6 (paper)

Marketed and Distributed outside the USA and Canada by Longman Group UK Limited, London

Contents

Preface

Migration has burst once again onto the international stage as significant numbers of people enter nation-states that have closed or are closing their immigration doors. Some 100 million people are living outside their countries of citizenship as legal immigrants, refugees and applicants for asylum, and illegal aliens. If collected into one nation, these migrants would be the world's tenth most populous country.

About half of this migrant nation is in the industrial democracies that are members of the OECD, and these nations are struggling to find responses to the problems that result. One remedy frequently proposed is to substitute flows of trade and investment for the migration of people from developing to industrial countries. Regional trade agreements such as the North American Free Trade Agreement (NAFTA), it is hoped, can accelerate economic growth in the sending countries and thus reduce migration or at least head off threatened increases.

Migration has not been a major concern of those interested in international trade and finance, or even in international relations more broadly, in recent years. However, the growing and seemingly uncontrolled movement of people has begun to affect international economic relations, as when the threat of unwanted immigration slows progress toward a border-free Europe; international politics, as when the United Nations establishes a sanctuary in Northern Iraq to avoid a flow of Kurdish refugees into Turkey; and domestic politics, as when antiforeigner attacks in Germany force the government to tackle difficult migration questions.

The Institute has therefore decided to look into the migration issue, and particularly to analyze its intersection with the other elements of international economic exchange. We do so initially in the context of one of the most controversial issues of contemporary American trade policy—NAFTA. The purpose of NAFTA is to reduce trade barriers and thereby stimulate economic and job growth throughout North America. But the major linkage between the United States and Mexico during the 20th century has been migration. One goal of NAFTA is to stimulate employment and wage growth in Mexico, which will eventually reduce that country's emigration pressures.

I asked Philip Martin, an agricultural economist at the University of California-Davis and an outstanding expert on migration issues throughout the world, to review the likely effects of NAFTA on Mexican migration to the United States. This study is the result of his effort. We hope that it will contribute both to the current debate on NAFTA and to a better understanding of the international economic (and other) ramifications of the migration issue more broadly.

The Institute for International Economics is a private nonprofit institution for the study and discussion of international economic policy. Its purpose is to analyze important issues in that area and to develop and communicate practical new approaches for dealing with them. The Institute is completely nonpartisan.

The Institute is funded largely by philanthropic foundations. Major institutional grants are now being received from the German Marshall Fund of the United States, which created the Institute with a generous commitment of funds in 1981, and from the Ford Foundation, the William and Flora Hewlett Foundation, the William M. Keck, Jr. Foundation, the C. V. Starr Foundation, and the United States–Japan Foundation. A number of other foundations and private corporations also contribute to the highly diversified financial resources of the Institute. About 16 percent of the Institute's resources in our latest fiscal year were provided by contributors outside the United States, including about 7 percent from Japan.

The Board of Directors bears overall responsibility for the Institute and gives general guidance and approval to its research program— including identification of topics that are likely to become important to international economic policymakers over the medium run (generally, one to three years), and which thus should be addressed by the Institute. The Director, working closely with the staff and outside Advisory Committee, is responsible for the development of particular projects and makes the final decision to publish an individual study.

The Institute hopes that its studies and other activities will contribute to building a stronger foundation for international economic policy around the world. We invite readers of these publications to let us know how they think we can best accomplish this objective.

C. FRED BERGSTEN
Director
September 1993

Acknowledgments

This monograph was begun in the Spring of 1992 while I was visiting the Institute. I am indebted to Howard Rosen, who arranged my Institute visit, Thomas O. Bayard, who insisted that it be completed almost on time, and C. Fred Bergsten, who shared his experience in searching for international solutions to difficult international problems.

Many people read and provided comments on all or part of the manuscript. Greg Schoepfle, Roger Böhning, Raul Hinojosa, Elizabeth Midgley, and Roger Kramer provided helpful comments, and the 40 participants in the December 8, 1992, Study Group meeting on the manuscript made a number of useful suggestions. Sidney Weintraub, Michael Teitelbaum, Jeffrey J. Schott, Gary Clyde Hufbauer, Demetrios Papademetriou, Howard Rosen, and Thomas O. Bayard read the entire manuscript carefully. Lee Knous cheerfully typed several versions.

Introduction

The North American Free Trade Agreement (NAFTA) was signed by the leaders of the United States, Canada, and Mexico on 17 December 1992. If ratified by the legislatures of these three countries, NAFTA will begin on 1 January 1994 to eliminate most tariff and nontariff barriers to trade between these three countries within 15 years. Reducing trade barriers should, in time, stimulate employment and economic growth in each country. Eventually, in the words of Mexican President Carlos Salinas de Gortari, "more jobs will mean higher wages in Mexico, and this in turn will mean fewer migrants to the United States and Canada. We want to export goods, not people" (quoted in letter President George Bush sent to Congress, 1 May 1991, p. 17).[1]

The purpose of NAFTA is to stimulate economic and job growth in Mexico, the United States, and Canada. Trade-stimulated economic growth should reduce emigration from Mexico: the US Commission for the Study of International Migration and Cooperative Economic Development (1990, 15–16) looked for "mutually beneficial, reciprocal trade and investment programs" to reduce unauthorized migration from Mexico and concluded that *"expanded trade between the sending countries and the United States is the single most important remedy"* (emphasis added) for unauthorized Mexico-to-US migration. However, the commission warned that "the economic development process itself tends in the short

---

1. In a 10 September 1992 speech to the Detroit Economic Club, President Bush said that the economic growth accelerated by NAFTA should "cut down on the cross-border flow of illegals that I think is burdening a lot of our country, particularly California."

to medium term to stimulate migration." Policies that accelerate economic growth—including privatization, land reform, and freer trade—produce a migration "hump", that is, temporarily more migration, creating a dilemma for a country such as the United States, which seeks to ratify free trade agreements and curb unauthorized immigration from Mexico. Accelerating development will eventually reduce migration, but "the development solution to unauthorized migration is measured in decades—even generations" (US Commission for the Study of International Migration and Cooperative Economic Development 1990, 36).

Migration humps are not new phenomena. The 48 million Europeans who emigrated from Europe between 1850 and 1925 represented about one-eighth of Europe's population in 1900, suggesting that "large-scale emigration was quite common during Europe's period of industrialization" (Massey 1991, 17). When southern European nations such as Italy and Spain industrialized and were integrated into the European Community (EC), their citizens, too, faced significant emigration pressures. However, during the 6 to 10 years Italians and Spaniards were waiting to be permitted to search freely for jobs throughout the EC, economic gaps narrowed, and few sought such employment (Straubhaar 1988). The migration hump also can be observed in Asia. Korea, for example, sent migrant workers to the Middle East and 25 percent more immigrants to the United States during the 1980s than it did during the 1970s, despite rapid economic growth during the 1980s (US Immigration and Naturalization Service, *Statistical Yearbook* 1990, 50).

A migration hump accompanies industrialization in countries with an emigration tradition or in which workers are recruited to go abroad. Mexico is such a country: as the world's major country of emigration, bordering on the world's major country of immigration, Mexico sent 3 million immigrants to the United States during the last decade, equivalent to 20 percent of Mexico's net population growth and 28 percent of legal US immigration (figure 1). Most of these Mexicans initially arrived illegally.[2]

This monograph investigates the reasons for, probable size, and likely duration of any NAFTA-stimulated increase in Mexico-to-US migration. It concludes that NAFTA will indeed contribute to a Mexico-to-US migration hump in the 1990s, just as the US migration commission predicted, because of NAFTA's effects on the three major variables that explain migration: demand-pull in the high-wage countries, supply-push in the

---

2. Between 1965 and 1992 some 21 million Mexicans were apprehended in the United States, while 3.7 million Mexicans became legal immigrants, including 2.2 million who became legal immigrants between 1989 and 1992. Apprehensions are events, not unique individuals, so that one person caught five times counts as five apprehensions. The probability of apprehension for an alien attempting illegal entry is about 30 percent (Acevedo and Espenshade 1992).

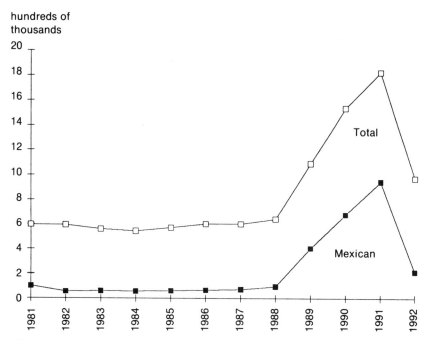

Figure 1 **Mexican and total legal immigration to the United States, 1981–92**

Source: Immigration and Naturalization Service, *Statistical Yearbook,* various years

low-wage countries, and personal and infrastructural networks linking immigrants to potential jobs. NAFTA's immediate effects on these variables are neutral or positive: it does not immediately reduce the pull of US jobs that attracts Mexican migrants; it adds to push factors, especially in rural Mexico; and it does not affect the strong networks that have evolved to link potential migrants in Mexico with jobs in the United States.

While it is relatively easy to project a short-term increase in Mexico-to-US migration because of NAFTA, it is very hard to predict how extensive this migration wave will be. European emigration involved over 10 percent of the population and persisted for decades while, in the case of southern Europe and Asia, migration humps involved less than 10 percent of the population and lasted less than two decades. It is unclear whether Mexico's growth path in light of changes in Mexican policies, NAFTA, and trends in the world economy will result in rapid 1960s Italian-style growth with declining migration or slower 19th century northern European growth with persisting emigration. The best analyses of NAFTA caution that Mexico's economic growth in the 1990s depends on many variables, including Mexico's ability to maintain stable fiscal and monetary policies and a continued expansion of world trade (Hufbauer and Schott 1992, 332–43).

If Mexico grows at 3 to 5 percent annually in the 1990s, more Mexicans can be expected to enter the United States as a result of faster labor displacement in rural Mexico, continued opportunity in the United States, and established networks that bridge the border.

The annual influx of legal Mexican immigrants over the next few years is expected to remain in the 100,000 to 150,000 range, and the number of temporary workers is expected to remain near 20,000 per year. Most Mexicans are expected to continue to arrive illegally; there are estimated to be 1.5 million to 2.5 million illegal entries each year, and over 90 percent of those apprehended are Mexicans. Yet these Mexicans are believed to be only one-third of the 300,000 illegal aliens who settle in the United States each year. The "base" level of total Mexico-to-US migration, then, involves 200,000 to 300,000 settlers annually, and 1.5 million to 2 million sojourners or temporary workers. If *more* Mexicans migrate to the United States as NAFTA is phased in, the NAFTA migration hump should be a small addition to an already significant flow. Unless the front door of legal immigration is opened wider, or a side door for temporary workers is available, this incremental influx is likely to arrive illegally. Most will return to Mexico after a short stay in the United States, but if NAFTA adds 10 percent to illegal entries and settlement, there could be 20,000 to 30,000 additional illegal Mexican immigrants annually.[3]

The strongest statement that can be made about NAFTA and migration is that the agreement is unlikely to reduce rising immigration immediately and is likely to contribute to the increase. However, the incremental immigration that can be attributed to NAFTA will be relatively small and limited in duration. The estimates reviewed in table 1 suggest that NAFTA and other Mexican policy reforms could bring up to several hundred thousand additional Mexican immigrants annually to the United States.

The situation in rural Mexico is a major factor behind these migration estimates: 28 million people there have per capita incomes that are only

---

3. The US has manipulated the means for entry on several occasions. In 1953–54, almost 2 million Mexicans were apprehended in order to encourage the employment of legal Braceros on US farms, and the Bracero side-door more than doubled in size between 1953 and 1956. Similarly, legal Mexican immigration averaged 67,000 per year between 1985 and 1987. The United States then had legalization programs that made over 2 million Mexicans legal immigrants. As a result, legal immigration from Mexico was 10 times higher (677,000) between 1989 and 1991.

Legal Mexican immigration will rise in the 1990s as some newly legalized immigrants unify their families here, and nonimmigrant flows should increase slightly with the expected increase in cross-border business and because 5,500 Mexican professionals are allowed to migrate to the United States as part of NAFTA. However, with 1 million new labor force entrants annually, including 300,000 to 400,000 in a shrinking Mexican agriculture, most 1990s Mexican immigrants are expected to arrive illegally, as they did in the 1980s.

Table 1 Projections of Mexico-to-US migration in the 1990s

Source	Migration projection	Period	Annual worker migration	Methodology	Reason for migration
Demographic models					
Garcia y Griego (1989)	200,000–500,000	1995–2000	n.a.	Regional demographic model	Demography
World Bank	750,000–900,000 Mexico to US	1995–2000	n.a.	Trend projection	Demography
Acevedo and Espenshade (1992)	1.1 million to 2.9 million gross undocumented Mexico-to-US flow	Annual flow	1.1 million to 2.9 million	Change from estimated baseline flow due to changing wages and unemployment ratios	Response in base flow due to relative labor market changes
CGE models					
Hinojosa-McCleery (1992)	Average stock of 0 to 5.5 million unauthorized Mexicans in the US	1986–2000	n.a.	Dynamic CGE model	NAFTA and US and Mexican policies
Levy and van Wijnbergen (1992)	700,000 displaced from agriculture due to trade liberalization	1 to 9 years	78,000	Dynamic CGE (Mexico only)	NAFTA and other trade liberalization policies
Robinson et al. (1991)	800,000 rural-urban migrants in Mexico; 600,000 migrants to US	1994–2000	100,000	Comparative statics; CGE	NAFTA and other Mexican policies
Other projections					
Calva (1992)	15 million displaced from Mexican agriculture	1990–2000	n.a.	Various	NAFTA and other Mexican policies
Tellez (1992)	Annual exit of 1 million from Mexican agriculture	1992–2002	n.a.	Various	NAFTA and other Mexican policies

CGE = computable general equilibrium
n.a. = not applicable

one-third of the country's $2,700 average, a tradition of migrating to the United States, and few prospects for NAFTA-stimulated job creation where they live. With projections that 20 to 50 percent of Mexico's farmers could leave the land over the next decade, the stage is set for a repeat of a great migration similar to what the United States experienced in the 1950s and 1960s, when structural changes in US agriculture and cotton harvest mechanization brought sharecroppers from Mississippi to Chicago. Mexico is on the verge of a similar agricultural revolution, but potential destination cities for ex-farmers include Los Angeles and Houston.

The evidence presented below suggests that NAFTA initially will add to Mexico-to-US migration, but that the incremental migration due to NAFTA could add perhaps only 10 percent to the flow, not 30 to 50 percent, as some other estimates suggest. A 10 percent increase in immigration would add about 30,000 Mexican settlers annually or, in terms of 1980s Mexican immigration, produce the equivalent of 11 years' immigration in 10 years.

This incremental migration is a reasonable price to pay for economic and trade policies that have elsewhere demonstrated their ability to convert Italy, Spain, and Korea, for example, from emigration to immigration nations. Furthermore, there is no credible alternative to NAFTA to eventually reduce Mexico-to-US migration pressures. However, policymakers should recognize and deal with the short-term migration hump so that migration does not become yet another obstacle to NAFTA ratification.

Migration has so far been ignored in the US debate over whether NAFTA should be approved. Mexico originally wanted to include migration in NAFTA negotiations, but US negotiators quickly got migration removed from the agenda. However, polls indicate that two-thirds of Americans want immigration reduced, and President Clinton in July 1993 announced proposals designed to reduce illegal immigration in the aftermath of the World Trade Center bombing and the smuggling of Chinese aliens into the United States. While these proposals did not target illegal immigration from Mexico, it will be hard to avoid discussing such migration from the major source country.

The migration hump is manageable, and addressing it can help to deal with larger illegal immigration issues. NAFTA should be implemented as scheduled, so as to lay the basis for the best-known cure for emigration pressure: economic growth. In addition, the federal government should take three steps to curb illegal immigration and to promote the integration of recently arrived immigrants. First, the United States should renew its commitment to enforce labor and immigration laws—lack of enforcement means that US jobs in agriculture, construction, and services continue to be a magnet for Mexican workers. Second, the United States and

Mexico should cooperate to reduce illegal entries and end the unparalleled massing of aliens at the border and the subsequent cat-and-mouse games with the US Border Patrol. Mexico could take steps to discourage such emigration by discouraging or prohibiting loitering at the border. Mexico and the United States might even experiment with a joint border patrol.

Closing the US labor market door and cooperating with Mexico to better control illegal border crossings can reduce the size of the migration hump, but such steps will neither eliminate illegal immigration nor help to integrate newcomers. Financially strapped state and local governments in the areas where most immigrants settle argue that the federal government has failed to keep its promise to help them integrate newcomers. Even if newcomers, on balance, pay more in taxes than they cost in government services, the evidence suggests that the federal government collects most of the taxes but provides few of the services. Federal immigration policy thus is analogous to trade policy in the sense that, despite national benefits, there are local costs, so that Migration Adjustment Assistance, analogous to Trade Adjustment Assistance, might be justified.

NAFTA is not the cause of rising Mexico-to-US migration, but it is a key ingredient in eliminating emigration pressures. It may not be fair to saddle a trade agreement with finding solutions to illegal immigration, but it appears that NAFTA has become a lightning rod for other issues that free trade may temporarily aggravate, such as environmental problems and the loss of US manufacturing jobs. NAFTA is likely to produce a temporary migration hump, but with NAFTA, there is likely to be less migration from Mexico over the next two decades than there would be without it. For this reason, NAFTA should be embraced as the best long-run solution to the persistent problem of Mexico-to-US migration.

Migration and Trade

1

The Quest for Immigration Control

The immigration problem has risen to the top of the international agenda because it defies an easy solution. For the first time, all of the major members of the Organization for Economic Cooperation and Development are countries of immigration. Many of the immigrants are unwanted, such as asylum applicants in Europe who are drawn there for economic reasons and unauthorized workers in the United States and Japan. The Group of Seven industrial nations declared in July 1991 that, although immigration in the past had been beneficial to both the migrants and their host societies, today's unpredictable waves of migrants have the potential to be both economically and politically destabilizing. As a result, the need to "do something" about immigration is a familiar refrain from Bonn to Tokyo.

There are two universally accepted ways to curb emigration pressures: promote economic development in emigration nations and foster political freedom and stability there. Economic development and growth, in turn, can be stimulated by freeing up trade and investment between richer and poorer nations and by the richer countries providing aid to their poorer neighbors. These external stimuli eventually reduce migration only if the developing nation adopts economic policies that reinforce its comparative advantages in the global economy.

Trade theory states that countries should produce those goods in which they have a comparative advantage. A country's comparative advantage, in turn, derives from its endowments of capital, labor, and resources, as well as its technology. Countries should export those goods that use intensively the factors in which they are relatively well-endowed and import those that intensively use those factors in which they are relatively poorly endowed. In a world of free trade, this theory predicts that labor-abundant emigration countries such as Mexico would send more labor-intensive tomatoes and fewer tomato pickers to the United States, or that trade could be a substitute for migration.

Demand-Pull Recruitment

Despite trade barriers and differences in wages and job opportunities, most people do not migrate. Migration is extraordinary; for this reason, most of today's unwanted migrations began with industrial-country programs that recruited workers from what became an emigration country. Once an industrial country sets worker migration in motion, the program acquires a life of its own, and policies in both emigration and immigration nations can reinforce the migration linkages between them.

Such an evolution describes Mexico-to-US migration. During the 1950s and 1960s, for example, the United States imported 4.6 million Mexican farm workers, and Mexico prohibited foreign investments in agriculture, encouraging the development in the United States rather than Mexico of labor-intensive farms that shipped fruits and vegetables long distances. Mexican trade policies relied on high tariffs and other barriers to discourage imports, and Mexico's overvalued peso discouraged exports. This "import-substituting industrialization" produced growth without jobs: the Mexican economy grew 6 percent annually during the 1950s, 1960s, and 1970s, but there was nonetheless considerable migration out of rural Mexico, where over half of the population lived in the 1960s. Rural Mexicans migrated both to Mexican cities and to the United States (Weintraub 1990b).

The United States did little to discourage the entry of rural Mexicans. The Mexican government recognized during the late 1940s that two Mexicans were entering the United States illegally for every Mexican who went as a legal participant in the Bracero program, and it urged the US government to negotiate an agreement that would channel Mexican workers into a legal program, where their rights could be protected. Indeed, the Mexican government tried to make a proposal to fine US employers who knowingly hired illegal aliens—its price for agreeing to the Bracero program in the early 1950s.[1] But the 1952 Immigration and Nationality Act, while making it unlawful to transport or "harbor" illegal aliens, explicitly defined harboring to exclude even the knowing employment of illegal aliens. This so-called Texas proviso meant that the worst

---

1. President Truman in 1951 aligned himself with the Mexican position: "Either punitive legislation aimed at halting the wetback flow would be enacted by Congress, or there would be no Bracero program" (Craig 1971, 94).

that would happen to US employers if they were discovered to be employing illegal workers was the removal of those workers.

When the Bracero program was ended in 1964, there were 1 million to 2 million Mexican men who had some experience working in the United States (Garcia y Griego 1981). As the US labor market tightened in the late 1960s and as US farmers learned that their ex-Braceros could become legal immigrants on the basis of letters that offered them jobs, thousands of ex-Braceros became immigrants. They showed their green US immigrant visas as they crossed the border, and these green-card commuters maintained the links that had been established between Mexican villages and US jobs.

These green-card commuters were in their 40s by the mid-1970s, and sons began to replace fathers in US fields. Young Mexicans were willing to migrate because there were few opportunities at home, and US employers faced no penalties for hiring them. As economic conditions deteriorated in Mexico and jobs remained available to Mexican workers in the United States, the number of illegal entries rose.

US and Mexican policies since the 1940s have created and sustained demand-pull factors in the United States and supply-push factors in Mexico. At the same time, networks permitted unauthorized migration from Mexico to surge in the 1980s. The United States tried—and failed—in 1986 to reduce Mexico-to-US migration by closing the labor market door to unauthorized workers with better border enforcement and fines on US employers who hired such workers (Bean, Edmonston, and Passel 1990; Fix 1991). Instead of curbing demand-pull pressures as expected, US immigration reforms strengthened the networks that link the US and Mexican labor markets (Commission on Agricultural Workers 1992). It is in this context—demand-pull recruitment initiated by the United States, supply-push pressures in rural Mexico, and networks that the US Immigration and Reform and Control Act of 1986 (IRCA) failed to break—that NAFTA's migration hump must be considered. Despite the hump, most migration specialists consider NAFTA the best long-run hope for eventually curbing Mexico-to-US migration (Bustamante, Reynolds, and Hinojosa-Ojeda 1992).

The European Immigration Crisis

European countries also set in motion demand-pull recruitment labor migration flows that have proved difficult to stop. During the 1960s, an unusual confluence of events created labor shortages in northern European nations. The number of new labor force entrants was low because of postwar privation, and it was difficult to persuade women in the 1960s to enter the labor market because of the delayed baby boom. Younger people were staying in school longer, while older workers retired earlier. With undervalued exchange rates, investment and export booms created so many jobs that, in the early 1960s, there were 10 vacant jobs for each unemployed worker in Germany.

Germany, France, and other northern European countries recruited guestworkers—ostensibly temporary workers from Italy, Turkey, and Algeria—who would learn about modern production methods while the savings they sent home were creating jobs to which they would return. In this mutually beneficial labor transfer, the availability of migrant workers sustained the economic boom in northern Europe by slowing inflationary pressures and minimizing labor market and economic adjustments. As presumably unemployed workers went abroad, emigration was expected to provide the jobs and remittances needed to accelerate growth and development in southern Europe (Kindleberger 1967).

The plan was to rotate guestworkers—to use them as a countercyclical tool of economic policy by importing workers during booms and exporting them during recessions. But guestworkers were legally probationary immigrants who could, after one year of satisfactory employment, renew their work and residence permits for two or three years and send for their families. After a second renewal, most were permanent residents who could remain with their families even if unemployed (Miller and Martin 1982). As a result, many guestworkers became permanent residents (Martin 1980). Most northern European countries stopped recruiting new guestworkers in 1973–74, but they permitted established workers to remain along with their families or to send for them. Employer sanctions, high unemployment rates, and repatriation programs combined to discourage entries and to prevent immigrant populations from surging in the 1970s.

Meanwhile, countries of emigration experienced diverging patterns of development. Mexico, Turkey, and North African emigration nations experienced growth without jobs. As a result, emigration pressures appeared to be rising during the 1980s. In the case of Turkey, for example, about 700,000 young men are believed to have left for Europe in the late 1960s and early 1970s, equivalent to almost 20 percent of the 20- to 35-year-old men in Turkey. When Turkey applied for EC membership in 1987, a survey of Turkish officials and returned guestworkers suggested that at least one-third of the young men, and many young Turkish women, would emigrate if they could; in other words, instead of the 1 million Turks registered to emigrate in 1973, almost 3 million would emigrate today if they could (Martin 1991, 94). Even though Europeans maintained that unskilled Turks would not find jobs, fears of a Turkish migration hump played an important role in the European Community's rebuffing of Turkey's application for membership in 1989.

As EC '92 measures accelerated economic and job growth in northern Europe and as emigration was permitted from Eastern Europe, there

Box 1 Germany: reluctant land of immigration

The Federal Republic of Germany does not consider itself to be a country of immigration, yet this may change: in 1990 more newcomers arrived there than in any other OECD country. The arrival in Germany of 1 million newcomers—ethnic Germans, relatives of immigrants already settled in Germany, applicants for asylum, and legal and illegal foreign workers—contributed to an anti-immigrant backlash that included over 2,300 attacks on foreigners in 1992.

Germany is a reluctant land of immigration in the sense that, although no immigrants are anticipated or planned for, almost 8 percent of the population is of foreign nationality. Immigration continues to add almost 1 percent annually to the German population, much of it in the form of applicants for asylum, who receive housing and living allowances while their cases are considered. After a difficult debate, Germany began on 1 July 1993 to turn back applicants for asylum who entered through a "safe" country where they could have applied, but international obligations, historical factors, and economic needs will make it difficult for Germany to bring immigration down to low levels quickly or easily.

Germany became a land of immigration in part because it pursued flawed policies that worked the first time they were tried. For example, when a recession in 1967 made guestworkers jobless, most left the country, reinforcing the theory that guestworkers could be rotated in and out of the labor market as needed. Similarly, when Germany first experienced a rush of asylum seekers in 1980, the crisis seemed to be solved merely by requiring entry visas of Turks, who were half of the 110,000 applicants for asylum. Neither rotating guestworkers nor using visas to restrict the number of asylum applicants proved effective.

Germany is today searching for durable immigration policies. In the 1990s, Germany is likely to enact an annual ceiling on the number of immigrants. Thus restrictionists will be able to say that 200,000 or 300,000 immigrants—but no more—can be admitted each year, while admissionists can proclaim that Germany is open to 200,000 or 300,000 newcomers. The first steps toward such a policy were taken in 1992, when Germany restricted to 225,000 annually the number of "ethnic Germans" in the former Soviet Union who can move to Germany as German citizens.

Accepting the reality of immigration nonetheless leaves Germans with many questions to resolve: how many, from where, and in what status newcomers should arrive.

Source: Martin (1993).

was a new wave of immigration (Martin, Hönekopp, and Ulmann 1990). Germany, with one-fourth of the EC economy, became the destination for half of these immigrants. Even though the German population is shrinking, Germany continues to proclaim that it is not a country of immigration, despite the fact that in 1990, Germany received 1 million newcomers—more than any other OECD country (box 1).

In Germany and elsewhere in Europe, controlling immigration is considered a top domestic priority. Migration that began as ostensibly mutually beneficial temporary worker programs has developed into an explosive political issue that may slow progress toward economic and political integration.

US Benign Neglect

In 1991 over 1.8 million immigrants and refugees were "admitted" to the United States. Only one-fourth of these immigrants were new arrivals; three-fourths were already here, and their status was adjusted to make them legal immigrants. In 1992 immigration returned to the more normal level of almost 1 million.

All people in the United States are either US citizens or aliens. Aliens are citizens of other countries. While in the United States, they fall into one of three categories: immigrants, nonimmigrants, and unauthorized or illegal aliens (box 2). The United States made major changes in its immigration laws during the 1980s, first enacting a Grand Bargain in 1986—awarding legal immigrant status to illegal aliens who had developed an equity stake in the United States and fining or imposing sanctions on employers who knowingly hired unauthorized workers. In 1990, with illegal immigration supposedly deterred and under pressure from the business community to make it easier for permanent and temporary immigrants with special skills to come to the United States, the legal immigration door was opened wider.

But illegal immigration continued. The 1991–92 recession, the abuse of the asylum procedure (through which aliens in the United States ask to stay to avoid persecution at home) and the addition of Chinese to the illegal alien flow have persuaded most Americans that new efforts should be made to reduce legal and illegal immigration. A *Wall Street Journal/* NBC poll in December 1992 found that 71 percent of those surveyed thought that immigration should be "cut back," and 55 percent of the Americans polled by Roper in April 1992 favored a moratorium on further immigration (18 December 1992, A1).

The United States is moving to restrict immigration in what appears to be an increasingly polarized debate. On the one side are organizations such as Federation for American Immigration Reform (FAIR), which argue that too many people are coming in. They call for a moratorium on immigration to reduce strains on the labor market and social services in heavily affected states such as California and to allow recent arrivals and Americans to adjust to each other. At the other extreme, the *Wall Street Journal* advocates a constitutional amendment stating that "there shall be open borders."[2] Immigration promises to be a major demo-

2. A *Wall Street Journal* editorial on 3 July 1986 first made this proposal, which was repeated in an editorial on 3 July 1990. Immigration proponent Julian Simon (1981, 275) argues that "admitting immigrants improves our standard of living."

Box 2 Immigrants, refugees, nonimmigrants, and unauthorized aliens

All US residents are either US citizens or aliens, who can be immigrants, refugees, nonimmigrants, or unauthorized.

Immigrants are citizens of other countries who have been granted a visa that allows them to live and work permanently in the United States and to become naturalized US citizens. Immigrant visas are normally issued to foreigners at US consulates in their home countries. Immigrants receive a US visa that, along with their foreign passport, entitles them to enter the United States. Once here, immigrants receive a card indicating their permanent resident status. This card used to be green, so that immigrants are still referred to frequently as "green-card holders."

Immigrants are admitted on the basis of family ties or professional or job qualifications. When the Immigration Act of 1990 is fully phased in, in fiscal 1995, the United States will admit up to 675,000 family and economic immigrants annually: 480,000, or 71 percent, will be family-sponsored; 140,000, or 21 percent, will be admitted to fill vacant US jobs; and 55,000, or 8 percent, will be "diversity" immigrants, primarily from European countries.

The number of *refugees* is determined annually by the president in consultation with Congress; this number was 132,000 in fiscal 1993 and is expected to be 120,000 in fiscal 1994. The number of *asylum applicants* depends on how many aliens request safe haven upon their arrival in the United States—over 100,000 recently. Many of these applications are denied, but an estimated 80 percent of those rejected nonetheless remain in the United States illegally.

There are also certain types of aliens who are in a transitional status. Legalized aliens, special agricultural workers, and Cuban-Haitian entrants are examples of temporary US categories that eventually permit aliens to become immigrants.

Nonimmigrants are granted temporary entry into the United States for a specific purpose, such as to visit, work, or study. There are many categories of nonimmigrants—each warranting a distinct US visa stamp. There were 21 million nonimmigrants admitted in 1992, including 16 million tourists and almost 3 million business visitors. There were 176,000 temporary foreign workers and 241,000 foreign students admitted in 1992. In addition, foreign government officials, people working in international organizations in the United States, foreign journalists, and NATO officials arrive in the United States as nonimmigrants.

Unauthorized aliens are those without immigrant or nonimmigrant visas. Most slip across the Mexico-US border. Others enter legally, say as a tourist, and then violate the terms of their entry by staying too long or by working in the United States.

graphic, economic, and political issue in the United States at the end of the 20th century, as it was at the beginning.

The debate between restrictionists and admissionists promises to heat up in the 1990s for three reasons. First, the number of immigrants is rising. Immigration has once again become a major contributor to population growth: about 40 percent of annual US population growth is due to the immigration of 1 million newcomers—the equivalent of adding a Dallas or Detroit every year.

Second, today's immigrants are diverse in their ethnicity, education, and skills. Earlier waves of immigrants were mostly Europeans who arrived in Eastern cities such as New York. Today's immigrants are primarily from Latin American and Asian countries, and they settle in the South and the West. The United States and most other industrial countries previously fostered diamond-shaped skill and income distributions, with most of the population in the middle classes. Today's immigrants help to move the United States from a diamond to more of an hourglass society: immigrants tend to be either professionals *or* unskilled workers—they are bunched near the extremes of the education and income spectrum.

Third, there is no consensus among politicians, researchers, or Americans on whether today's immigrants will be assets or liabilities tomorrow. The success of some immigrants in business and education suggests that the nation will reap a windfall due to today's immigration, while other income, education, and public assistance data suggest that the United States may be directly and indirectly expanding its underclass (Borjas 1990).

The US debate on whether to renew efforts to control illegal immigration and to reduce legal immigration often takes advocates back to fundamental questions, such as how much immigrant workers affect US labor markets and economic growth. Immigrants contributed about one-fourth of US labor force growth in the 1980s, and at current rates they are expected to contribute one-third to work force growth in the 1990s. If immigrants exactly replicated the US labor force in education, skills, and earnings, then their arrival might slow the rate of increase in wages, because more workers are available, but it would not affect the difference in wages between, for example, autoworkers and janitors. However, since immigrants cluster at the ends of the education and earnings spectrum, they add—marginally—to earnings inequality.

The bimodal skills and earnings of contemporary immigrants make it hard to conduct an overall assessment of the effects of immigrants on the United States. Businesses and universities often seek highly educated Asian engineers and scientists, and these immigrants probably raise the productivity of the US economy and average incomes. Mexican farm workers with little schooling, on the other hand, are desired because farmers believe they are the only group available to harvest fruits and vegetables. However, if immigrant farm workers are readily available, farmers have little incentive to improve wages and working conditions in order to attract American workers or to move production to Mexico and other areas with farm workers.

American history and experience place high hurdles in front of those who would restrict immigration to the United States. Furthermore, recent patterns of Mexico-to-US migration make control even more difficult. Unlike trade channels, immigration channels widen over time.[3] In addition, there is often a large gap between immigration policy goals and outcomes. The United States abolished the national origins system for selecting immigrants in 1965 amidst predictions that the predominantly European origins of immigrants would not change, although Europeans and Canadians went from two-thirds of the immigrants who arrived in the 1950s to one-fourth of those who arrived in the 1970s. Similarly, the United States tackled but failed to resolve three major immigration issues during the 1980s: refugees, illegal aliens, and legal immigrants.

Immigration has in the past occurred in waves, which implies peak-and-trough inflows. It is not clear how much time (if any) societies need to absorb a peak or how long the past immigration pauses would have to have been to produce a consensus in 2050 that today's immigration was in the national interest. In the past, two or three decades of rising immigration has been followed by several decades of little immigration.

It is this last point—the breathing space that followed past waves of immigrants—that has become an issue today in areas such as California (box 3). The state's population has been growing by 2.5 percent annually, with half of this growth due to immigration. The arrival of over 1 million immigrants and refugees during the 1980s gave California a population growth rate faster than that of Mexico and comparable to that of Morocco. If California continues to get its present share of legal and illegal entries, then the state's population of 31 million today will be 38 million to 40 million in 2000.

Most immigrants to California are Hispanics and Asians. Some are professionals, but most are unskilled. During the 1980s, their arrival demonstrated the extraordinary economic and job growth that can be achieved with a first-world infrastructure and a third-world labor force (Muller and Espenshade 1985). Los Angeles, for example, emerged as the nation's largest manufacturing center for both high-tech aerospace and related industries and for the low-wage garment, shoe, and furniture

---

3. Immigration is in this sense different from trade. Trade channels tend to narrow over time as "special interests" seek protection from imports, so periodic rounds of trade negotiations seem necessary to keep trade channels open and widening. Immigration channels between more- and less-developed economies, by contrast, seem to widen and deepen over time if government does not restrict them.

Box 3 California: Wave of the future?

California is home to 11 percent of the US population, one-third of the legal immigrants to the United States, and one-half of the illegal immigrants. Legal and illegal immigrants continued to arrive in the early 1990s, despite the state's worst recession in 50 years.

As a result, immigration has become a major political issue in the state. Governor Pete Wilson in January 1993 argued that 10 percent of the state's $50 billion budget was spent on legal and illegal immigrants, and he asked the federal government to reimburse $1.45 billion of these costs. According to Wilson, California's "quality of life is threatened by [the] tidal wave of illegal immigrants" (*Davis Enterprise*, 29 August 1993, A9).

During the 1980s, debates over illegal immigration centered on their labor market impacts. The Council of Economic Advisers (1986, 221) summarized the debate as follows:

> Although immigrant workers increase output, their addition to the supply of labor. . . [causes] wage rates in the immediately affected labor market [to be] bid down. . . Thus, native-born workers who compete with immigrants may experience reduced earnings or reduced employment.

Econometric studies that investigated these relationships, however, could "not detect a single shred of evidence that immigrants have a sizeable adverse impact on the earnings and employment opportunities of natives in the United States" (Borjas 1990, 81; Abowd and Freeman 1991). Some economists did not accept this conventional wisdom (Briggs 1984; 1992). They maintained that legal and illegal immigrants who concentrate in particular areas and industries should, according to economic theory, depress wages and displace workers as the CEA statement suggests. The failure of econometric studies to find these effects, they argued, was due more to imperfect data than to their absence. Indeed, some of those who once asserted that legal and illegal immigrants have no effect on unskilled American workers have changed their position: George Borjas, for example, says that while "in the 1980s, there was no evidence that immigration had [a negative labor market] impact, there is beginning to be evidence that there is such a impact" (*Sacramento Bee*, 29 August 1993, A4).

The 1990s debate over illegal immigration is focused on its public finance impacts. Governor Wilson noted that two-thirds of the babies born in Los Angeles public hospitals have illegal alien parents; he recommended that

industries. What was remarkable about this economic growth is that Mexican shoe makers who could not find jobs in Mexico's shoe industry came to Los Angeles to make shoes there.

Such immigration patterns reinforce other factors that promote economic inequality by adding proportionately more workers to the lowest-paying industries.[4] At the top, immigrant scientists and engineers fuel

---

4. Many studies note the growing inequality in earnings. Between 1979 and 1987, the real incomes of college graduates climbed by 33 percent, while the real incomes of high school graduates fell by 11 percent.

the US constitution be amended to stop granting these babies US citizenship. Wilson estimates that California spends $3 billion annually to provide health, education,and social services to illegal immigrants because of federal government mandates, so that the federal government should either reimburse states for these service costs or repeal the mandate that these services be provided.

Studies of the public finance impacts of illegal immigrants reach different conclusions, but they agree on one point: the taxes that young and unskilled illegal immigrants pay flow to the federal government, while the services they use tend to be paid for by state and local taxes. In Los Angeles County, for example, 2.3 million people—25 percent of the population—are recent legal and illegal immigrants. These immigrants paid an estimated $4.3 billion in taxes in 1991–92 and led to county costs for health and justice services of $947 million. However, the federal government received 60 percent of the taxes these immigrants paid, and the county only 3 percent, leaving the county with an $808 million public finance gap (Los Angeles County 1992, 3–9). A San Diego study concluded that illegal immigrants in that county led to a $150 million public finance deficit (Auditor General of California 1992).

Some of the assumptions used in these studies have been criticized. For example, should the illegal-immigrant share of the arrests or imprisonments (15 percent in San Diego) be their share of justice costs, or should it be assumed that, even if there were no illegal immigration there would be a justice system, so that only the marginal cost of illegal immigrants should be considered? However, most studies of the public finance impacts of legal and illegal immigrants agree that their taxes tend to flow to the federal government, while their service costs tend to be paid by state and local governments.

These studies and state and local government "bills" for federal reimbursement have led to slightly more federal moneys for immigrant integration and a spate of federal and state proposals to reduce illegal immigration. Among these proposals, those that call for a $1 border crossing toll could generate $150 million annually for enforcement measures if US citizens and aliens continue to cross the US-Mexican border at the present rate. Other proposals would deny drivers' licenses to illegal aliens, require health care providers expecting reimbursement to report suspected illegal aliens to the US INS, and encourage illegal-alien felons to serve their sentences in their home countries, with US state governments paying the tab.

the growth of the nation's well-paid education and high-technology industries; they may also help to restrain wage increases for such workers. At the bottom, immigrant farm workers and laborers help to hold down wages and thus prices for fruits and vegetables and gardening services. The growing economic inequality is not mitigated by social service programs, which in an era of budget shortages are shrinking. In California, the gap between the priorities of the older whites, who cast most of the votes in elections, and young minority immigrants, who often do not vote, has been described as an important factor in making the state a unique laboratory in which to determine whether the world's first "universal" nation can function effectively.

Asia: Dawn of a Guestworker Era?

Asian countries such as Japan did not recruit migrant workers in the 1950s and 1960s as other industrial countries did. However, these nations, which seem to have taken as many jobs to workers as possible, may now have to begin importing workers to fill jobs. Japan has at least 500,000 legal and illegal migrant workers, and Hong Kong, South Korea, Taiwan, and Singapore are initiating or expanding guestworker programs to legalize growing influxes of illegal migrant workers (Martin 1991). If Japan were to permit European levels of foreign worker employment, the number of migrant workers could rise to 5 million (box 4).

Most of the Asian industrial nations experiencing immigration pressures have announced programs to manage what some see as inevitable immigration, and others argue that this is a threat to the ethnic and cultural homogeneity that they believe made them economically successful. As a result, their new immigration programs avoid the conversion of temporary workers into permanent residents that occurred in the United States and in Europe.

During the late 1980s, when there were few opportunities for worker entries, no employer sanctions, and agreements with countries such as Iran and Bangladesh that permitted visa-free entry, migrant workers began to arrive in Japan as tourists and then go to work. Over 14,000 such workers were apprehended in 1988, a sixfold increase over 1982. Based on the gap between foreigners arriving and departing Japan, there are almost 300,000 who have overstayed, virtually all of whom are thought to be illegal workers. Three-fourths of these are from six countries: Thailand, Korea, Malaysia, Philippines, Iran, and China. Other estimates put the number of illegal workers at 500,000 or more.

After an initial panic in 1990, when Japanese employers, fearing big fines, fired illegal alien workers, it soon became apparent that fines would be the exception, not the rule. It appears that there are no more than 10 to 20 employer fines annually. Immigration law enforcement has a unique Japanese twist: 90 percent of the apprehensions are foreigners who turn themselves into immigration authorities in order to get the exit stamp that is needed to leave the country. Instead of fining these aliens or their employers, immigration authorities usually process them for deportation, so that illegal alien employment in Japan ends with a quiet one-way ticket home.

Foreign students and illegal aliens proved to be insufficient to fill the number of employer requests for unskilled workers. Instead of resolving the divisive issue of whether Japan should import unskilled foreign workers, the Japanese government revised its foreign trainee program in 1992. The ban on unskilled workers remains in place, but employers willing to train unskilled foreign workers in Japan can apply to a new organization—the Japan International Training Cooperation Organiza-

Box 4   Japan: a Pacific destiny for immigrants?

Japan is an economic power confronting an immigration dilemma: should the industrial world's number-two economy admit immigrant workers during the 1990s? Among the major OECD countries, Japan has the fewest foreigners in its population and work force.

The Japanese government acknowledged the problem of illegal immigration in 1990 by enacting a law that fines employers up to 2 million yen ($20,000) for hiring illegal aliens. The Japanese government also ended visa-free entry for Iranians, Pakistanis, and Bangladeshis, countries that sent a significant number of "tourists" to Japan who went to work illegally.

About 1.2 million foreigners, half Koreans, are living legally in Japan. The legal foreign population in Japan rose about 50 percent during the 1980s, but the number of illegal foreigners increased over 10-fold to at least 300,000. Japan is debating whether its "one people, one nation" adherence to ethnic homogeneity is more important than projections that the country will need to import 500,000 to 2 million foreign workers by 2000 to avert labor shortages.

The Japanese government's policy toward foreign workers is based on three principles. First, foreign workers are to be admitted only as a last resort. Second, unskilled immigrants should be avoided in order to minimize social problems and to avoid preserving sunset industries. Third, foreign workers should not settle in Japan.

A two-tiered policy has evolved that at least partially belies these principles. First, beginning in 1993, restrictions on permanent foreign residents (including second- and third-generation Koreans) were eased, and the presence in Japan of about 150,000 of the 1.5 million Latin Americans of Japanese descent was recognized. These new policies run counter to practices of closely checking employer requests to hire foreign workers, regulating the skills of those who enter, and discouraging settlement.

Second, employers have successfully pressed the Japanese government to let them employ foreign students and trainees. There are 48,000 foreign college students in Japan and 35,000 foreigners learning Japanese. Both may work up to 4 hours daily and 28 hours weekly, although the Chinese students of Japanese in particular appear to view the $3,000-$4,000 tuition fee as the cost of a Japanese work permit. This perspective has been borne out when, in several instances, the Japanese language schools to which the tuition was paid closed soon after students with 6- or 12-month work-study visas arrived.

The major Japanese response to labor shortages has been to introduce a trainee program. Unskilled foreigners cannot be employed as workers in Japan, but they can work in Japanese factories for two years as they acquire training that should be useful after they return to China or the Philippines. Trainees initially work two hours for each hour they study, but after three to six months, they may engage in full-time on-the-job "training" (i.e., working). The number of trainees has tripled since 1986 to 45,000, and admitting 400,000 to 500,000 trainees in Japan to the mid-1990s is under discussion.

tion (JITCO)—for permission to bring trainees to Japan. JITCO, in turn, is to establish centers in China, the Philippines, and other emigration countries at which trainees would register for two-year work-and-learn stints in Japan. After two years, the JITCO centers that recruited them would help to place returning trainees in jobs in their home countries.

The trainee program appears to be a rapidly expanding nonimmigrant guestworker program. There were 14,000 foreign trainees in Japan in 1986, 38,000 in 1990, and 43,000 in March 1993. There is no countrywide quota on the number of trainees, and current government plans envision expanding to 100,000 new entrants annually.[5] However, business leaders, who predict that they will be 2 million to 3 million workers short by the turn of the century and 10 million workers short when Japan's population is projected to peak at 130 million in 2010, talk of many more trainees—at least 400,000 to 500,000 in the mid-1990s.

The Japanese government has already modified the trainee program in ways that make it more similar to a contract worker program. In April 1993, the government permitted trainees to be considered "workers" after being certified. Worker-trainees can be requested by name—and most are—but they cannot bring their families to Japan, and the intent is to enforce rotation strictly after two years.

Japan is walking a tightrope. On the one hand, the Japanese see the need for transitional foreign workers—they are intended to offer small employers a helping hand until automation at home or investment abroad makes foreign workers unnecessary. On the other, they recognize that the availability of foreign worker trainees reduces incentives to automate and invest abroad, but they hope to imitate Singapore and nonetheless regulate the behavior of both their own employers and foreign workers.

In Asia, the most ethnically homogeneous countries have been slowest to open themselves to foreign workers: Singapore and Malaysia, for example, opened themselves to immigrants long before Japan, South Korea, and Taiwan. Most Japanese do not want to turn the country into an immigration destination, and some economists (Shimada 1993) note that if Japan in the 1990s accepts unskilled migrant workers, the impetus for economic restructuring may be lost. These critics note that Japanese companies often require workers to leave their jobs at 55, that relatively few Japanese women are in the work force, and that many Japanese service businesses are "overstaffed" by international standards.

---

5. There are firm-specific quotas: trainees can be up to 5 percent of a company's labor force. But small companies with fewer than 50 employees are entitled to three foreign trainees, so that, a company with, for example, one Japanese employee and three foreign trainees could have 75 percent trainees. Foreign workers in small companies are regulated by local employer associations.

Development and Migration

Demand-pull recruitment played a significant role in setting current world south-to-north migration flows in motion. Network factors range from the export of movies and television programs that raise expectations abroad to an expansion of civil and social rights for all residents of industrial countries (Hollifield 1992); these have made the job of controlling immigration far more difficult. Since it seems difficult to reduce demand-pull factors quickly, or to manage network factors, OECD countries have recently expressed a renewed interest in growth-promoting aid and trade measures that might accelerate development and thus reduce supply-push emigration pressures.

Development has reduced emigration pressures on many occasions, but its effects have often not been felt for decades. The migration transition for some countries in southern Europe and Asia was very rapid by historical standards. For example, Italian labor migration to northern Europe peaked in the early 1960s, when almost 5 percent of Italy's 20 million workers were employed abroad. However, slow population growth, the rapid transformation of agriculture, and the Italian economic miracle created jobs and raised wages so that, when Italians got the right to seek jobs on an equal footing with other workers throughout the European Community, few did (Böhning 1972). For the same reasons, Greece, Spain, and Portugal also sent few workers north. Similarly, South Korea went from being a major labor exporter in the early 1980s to a major labor importer a decade later.

The European experience with development shows that the migration hump can be short-lived. Furthermore, income and unemployment gaps do not have to disappear to stop migration: the per capita income gap between Portugal and France, and between Greece and Germany, is about 1-to-4, and unemployment rates are at least twice as high in southern EC emigration countries.

Development can reduce emigration pressures, but it need not do so (Appleyard 1989). Puerto Ricans as US citizens have the right to migrate to the US mainland, and despite rapid economic growth and the creation of a social safety net on the island, Puerto Ricans continue to emigrate to the US mainland. Like Mexico, Turkey changed to an export- and market-oriented economic policy in the 1980s that produced rapid economic growth but few new jobs and falling real wages (Adler 1981), so that the emigration areas of the 1960s still had significant pent-up emigration pressures a decade later (Abadan-Unat et al. 1976; Paine 1974). The European Community had in the 1960s signed agreements with Turkey that anticipated development sufficient to permit freedom of movement for Turks by the mid-1970s. This migration provision did not come into force, and although Turkish emigration to the European Community was sharply curtailed in 1973, EC nations such as Germany and the Netherlands feared that Turkey had not made enough development progress to prevent a significant migration hump. The European Community rebuffed Turkey's application for membership in 1989.

If Turkey had been accepted into the European Community, would there have been a migration hump? During the time that Turkey's application was being considered, the migration issue was framed by two extreme scenarios (Martin 1991). The stay-at-home scenario emphasized the anticipated absence of pull factors in Europe that might stimulate Turkish emigration, noting that Turkish migration to Europe was stopped in the 1980s by high unemployment rates for unskilled workers and by new immigration controls. Even if Turkish unemployment after 2000 were two or three times northern European levels, and even if Turkish wages remain at one-tenth European levels, unskilled Turks would migrate to Europe, this scenario ran, only to engage in an expensive and fruitless job search. When the word got out that there were no jobs, even this exploratory migration would end.

The alternative scenario emphasized Turkish push factors and a Say's Law notion that readily available unskilled workers will eventually make a place for themselves even in highly-regulated labor markets. Unemployment and underemployed in Turkey worsened during the 1980s despite the fact that Turkey had some of the fastest economic growth rates among OECD countries. Its workers, free to seek jobs throughout the European Community, would, according to this argument, soon make a place for themselves in agriculture, construction, and service industries that depend on migrant workers.

The most reasonable scenario is to expect an initial rise in migration, followed by a level of migration congruent with the evolution of the European labor market. If jobs were available in northern Europe, then the likely annual entry of 600,000 to 800,000 new workers into a Turkish labor market that has traditionally created 200,000 to 300,000 jobs would likely produce significant emigration. Although this migration hump was widely acknowledged, few researchers or officials were willing to speculate on the size and duration of the migration hump or any continuing level of migration (Martin 1991).

The Puerto Rican and Turkish models of development and continued emigration pressures may be more appropriate for Mexico than the southern European models of economic integration without migration. Like Puerto Ricans, Mexicans have had fairly free access to the United States for decades, and as a result there are strong networks in place that permit Mexicans to respond to demand-pull and supply-push factors despite border barriers.[6] Like Turkey, Mexico in the 1980s changed its

---

6. Note that Europeans believe they can control immigration from a country such as Turkey until Turks are granted freedom-of-movement rights. A recent review of how Turkish accession might affect the EC labor supply noted that even though pressures to emigrate from Turkey are rising, "there is no great scope for additional Turkish immi-

economic policies, and the result has been rapid economic growth but not enough jobs, falling real wages, and rural-urban migration (Weintraub 1990b).

The European Community looked at Turkey and postponed negotiations for Turkish economic and political integration; the United States, by contrast, embraced Mexico's request for a more limited economic integration. The North American Free Trade Agreement (NAFTA) will test how fast emigration pressures can be reduced with a fairly narrow form of economic integration.

Trade and Migration

The relationship between development and migration has been described as "unsettled" and "uncertain" (Papademetriou and Martin 1991; Penninx 1982), but there is much more literature exploring this relationship than there is on the linkage between trade and migration. There is a fairly simple explanation for this disparity: trade theory asserts that factor prices or wages tend toward equality, so that trade *or* migration can reduce economic incentives for migration. Since trade theorists usually assume, with Adam Smith, that "man is of all sorts of luggage the most difficult to be transported," they usually assume that labor does not cross national borders. Instead, trade theorists concentrate on how free trade in goods makes labor migration unnecessary (Straubhaar 1988, 18–22).

The Migration Hump

The prediction that free trade eventually reduces wage differences between countries and thus reduces labor migration between them rests on several assumptions. Mundell (1957), for example, assumed that two countries have different factor endowments and common technologies. If there is full employment in both countries and migration is motivated by wage differences, then even if trade in goods is restricted, there will be only a migration hump as labor flows across borders to equalize wages and then no more economically motivated migration. Trade protectionism, according to theory, does not eliminate the migration hump, but "labor mobility [can] fully compensate for the non-traded good" (Krauss 1976, 474).

Protectionism produces a migration hump, according to the following scenario. Beginning with free trade, if the United States levies or raises tariffs on Mexican fruits and vegetables, US farm wages should initially

---

grants," reinforcing the belief that EC countries can control entries over their borders (Hönekopp 1992, 73).

rise as US prices for fruits and vegetables rise under the cover of tariff protection. If there is an opportunity to migrate, Mexican workers would then enter the United States in response to these higher wages. Their exit from Mexico should raise wages and prices there, and Mexico-to-US migration should eventually eliminate the incentive to trade fruits and vegetables. In this manner, moving from free trade to protection should lead to a migration hump followed by no migration.

If common technologies and different labor endowments lead to the proposition that trade impediments can cause labor migration, then the corollary is that free trade should eventually reduce labor migration. However, there is virtually no theory of how the path to free trade is likely to affect migration. There are only examples, none of which are directly applicable to the Mexico-US relationship. The unification of Germany provides one. Despite government efforts to reduce wage gaps and thus deter economic migration, there was an east-to-west migration hump in 1989–90, and migration is expected to continue at 300,000 to 400,000 annually during the 1990s (Hönekopp 1992, 6–9). History provides another example. Thomas (1973) argued that migration flows across the Atlantic in the 19th and 20th centuries mirrored the ratio of real wages in the old and new worlds: rising real wages in the United States relative to Europe led to more migration.

The argument for a migration hump as a result of freer trade between rich and poor nations that have an established migration relationship ultimately rests on the logic that free trade has positive or neutral effects on the three variables that govern migration. The closest theory for such an effect would be a Lewis-type development model (see Kindleberger 1967, chapters 1–2) in which there is a perfectly elastic supply of labor in the poor country willing to work in the rich country at prevailing wages there. Free trade can alter the job search calculus: wage differences between areas and sectors can change, encouraging rural-urban migration, for example, and if foreign investment creates jobs in urban areas or export zones, the probability of finding a job there could rise. These two factors in combination might encourage more individuals to migrate (Todaro 1969). Comparative static analysis eventually rules, and as economic differences narrow, labor migration decreases. In retrospect, this poor- to rich-country migration would appear as a short-term hump.

This short-term hump within a country is usually described as permanent rural-urban migration. Between countries, the migration hump can involve temporary or permanent migrants. Whether the hump migrants turn out to be temporary or permanent depends on host-country policies and conditions and sending-country growth. The Italian migration hump to northern Europe in the early 1960s resulted in a settled population there of over 1 million people, or 2 percent of Italy's population, even though most of the Italians who migrated north eventually returned.

	Trade patterns	Trade policies
Migration patterns	**A** Migration and trade can be *substitutes*, so that barriers to trade increase migration and freer trade reduces migration. Trade and migration can be *complements* if technologies differ, so that specialists migrate to service complex equipment.	**B** Migration creates a dependence on an external labor market for which trade and investment policies try to create a local substitute, e.g., the maquiladora program.
Migration policies	**C** Importing workers can be a decision not to import goods from the emigration country. However, migrant worker remittances can be spent on goods produced in the country of employment, thereby increasing trade.	**D** Trade policy exceptions can lead to migration policy exceptions, as when protections for the US sugar industry justify the H-2A foreign farm worker program. Immigration policy exceptions can increase trade, as when the admission of sports stars or music groups increases imports of equipment or records.

Figure 2 Four trade and migration linkages

There appears to be a difference in the nature of migration and economic integration between economically similar and different economies. Economic integration between economies at similar levels of development, such as between the United States, Europe, and Japan, seems to be associated with higher levels of nonimmigrant flows and lower levels of immigration. Economic integration between developing and industrial nations, as is envisioned between the United States and Mexico, seems to be marked by a migration hump.

Four Interactions

Trade theory has focused mainly on the extent to which migration is a substitute or complement for trade—box A of the four possible trade and migration linkage (figure 2). Box A interactions explain why NAFTA should eventually mean less Mexico-to-US migration, as Mexican tomatoes are substituted for Mexican tomato pickers in the United States, and why NAFTA should prompt more American professionals and specialists to migrate to Mexico to sell and service the increased quantity of goods that are expected to be sold there.

The other trade and migration interactions have not received as much attention, in part because some are extensions of box A. Perhaps the most studied case is box D, where a trade policy exception leads to a migration policy exception or vice versa. In some cases, eliminating these exceptions would allow trade and migration to be substitutes; in other cases, they would be complements.

A frequently cited example of substitutes is the US trade policy decision to protect US sugar growers by limiting imports so that the domestic US sugar price is maintained at a predetermined level. About half of US-grown sugar is from sugarcane, and over half of the sugarcane is produced in Florida. Sugarcane in Florida has been hand-harvested since the early 1940s, in 1990 with about 10,000 foreign workers. Most of these temporary alien workers are from Jamaica, a country whose ability to export sugar to the United States has been reduced because of rising US sugar production and thus a smaller export quota for emigration countries such as Jamaica. The so-called H-2A program through which these migrant cane cutters have been admitted to the United States is very controversial, with critics routinely alleging that the US government too easily permits US farmers to import "captive" foreign workers rather than adjust wages and working conditions so that Americans would cut the cane. With free trade in sugar, there would presumably be more sugar production and jobs in Jamaica, thus reducing emigration pressures there, and less demand for Jamaican sugarcane cutters in the United States. Alternatively, maintaining protection for US sugar but denying growers access to H-2A workers might cause wages in Florida to rise enough to justify the mechanization of the harvest. Machines harvest sugarcane in Louisiana and Hawaii, and in 1993, in response to a settlement in which growers agreed to change the method by which to establish rates for hand-cutting cane, machines now harvest a majority of Florida's crop.

In this case, a protectionist trade policy led to an immigration policy exception. Immigration policies also increase trade in a complementary fashion. The admission to the United States of foreign soccer and hockey players undoubtedly increases imports of sports equipment, just as the admission of foreign artists and entertainers may expose Americans to them and increase imports of their products. In these cases, expanding immigration tends to expand trade in complementary products.

Many industrial countries recruited guestworkers during the 1960s. Box C of figure 2 depicts the interaction between a policy to import workers and its effects on trade patterns. Overall, a US decision to import Mexican workers should reduce trade, since the US industry in which they are employed presumably expands so that there is less room for imports of that product. But migrant workers earn wages in the United States, and they remit on average only 40 percent of their earnings to Mexico (Ascencio 1993). Some of the remittances sent to Mexico are in turn spent on goods and services imported from the United States. If one-third of at least $75 billion in worldwide remittances are spent on goods imported from the industrial countries, then $25 billion in industrial-to developing-country trade would be traceable to migrant remittances.

Finally, figure 2 box B illustrates how trade policies can change in response to migration patterns. One example is on the US-Mexican border. Some of the Bracero farm workers who migrated seasonally to the United States moved their families to Mexican border cities, where they lived off remittances. When the United States terminated the program in 1964, there were several million Mexicans in border areas who could no longer depend on US earnings. Mexico responded with the maquiladora program in 1965, under which US investors could operate border-area plants and pay US duties only on the value added by Mexican workers as they turned imported components into finished products for US consumers. The maquiladora program was a trade and investment response to the termination of a temporary worker program.

The most fundamental trade and migration interaction is that in which trade is generally a substitute for migration. Among industrial countries, trade and nonimmigrant labor flows appear to be complements. When there is economic integration between industrial and developing nations, the theory suggests that there will be a migration hump. The other boxes in figure 2 outline policy-pattern interactions that illustrate how trade and migration can be substitutes or complements. While suggestive of the complexity of trade and migration, these other interactions tend to be extensions of the basic model.

Migration Trajectories

The basic model and its extensions can indicate whether trade and migration will be substitutes or complements, but they have difficulty predicting the magnitude and duration of the expected migration hump. This adjustment path is what is most important for evaluating the effects of NAFTA on Mexico-to-US migration.

There is little in theory or experience to suggest the dimensions of a Mexico-to-US migration hump. European Community countries integrated economically without much migration, but this is easily explained. First, the gaps between countries were not too far apart at the outset. Second, there were opportunities to emigrate under controlled programs, and immigration controls were fairly effective. Third, the economic gap between emigration and destination areas narrowed very quickly.

Put in terms of the more familiar demand-pull, supply-push, and network framework, the demand-pull for foreign workers to work in Northern Europe persisted after Italians got freedom-of-movement rights in 1968, but supply-push pressures fell so rapidly that there was little incentive to follow established migration networks to Northern Europe. In the cases of Greece, Spain, and Portugal, demand-pull was largely eliminated 10 to 15 years before workers got freedom-of-movement rights, and supply-push factors dissipated enough—by 1988 in the case of Greece and 1992 for Portugal and Spain—to prevent any sort of migration hump.

Does history and European experience teach that free trade can act as a substitute quickly enough so that there will generally be far less labor migration than one might expect? The answer is not necessarily, because NAFTA represents a type of economic integration that has not yet been attempted: NAFTA is the first attempt to substitute a trade and investment interaction for a migration linkage, and it seeks to achieve this substitution without dealing directly with current migration patterns or policies. Since there is no experience and insufficient data to formulate a reliable model of past, current, or future Mexico-to-US migration, the approach adopted here is to examine the likely evolution of demand-pull, supply-push, and network factors in the United States and Mexico in the 1990s. It should be possible to determine the effect of NAFTA on the sign of each of these determinants of migration and then to make an overall assessment of how NAFTA is likely to affect migration.

Before turning to the effects of NAFTA on migration, chapter 2 provides summary data on the NAFTA economies, reviews studies of the trade and labor effects of NAFTA, and summarizes predictions of Mexico-to-US migration. Chapter 3 traces the evolution of Mexican migration to the United States. It emphasizes that the neat match between demand-pull factors in the United States and supply-push factors in Mexico permitted networks to be forged over decades. Chapters 4, 5, and 6 highlight the likely effects of NAFTA on US demand-pull, Mexican supply-push, and network factors, respectively. The analysis indicates that this match is likely to persist in the 1990s. The analysis emphasizes the effects of these variables on agriculture in the two countries, since rural Mexicans have traditionally migrated for jobs in US agriculture.

The likely evolution of demand-pull, supply-push, and network factors suggest that NAFTA will accelerate displacement in rural Mexico and that networks paradoxically strengthened by US immigration reforms will guide some displaced workers to the United States. Chapter 7 examines a possible substitute or complement for this expected migration hump: maquiladoras, or foreign-financed operations in northern Mexico. The data on whether such operations are a stepping stone to the United States or help to stop such migration are reviewed.

Chapter 8 concludes that NAFTA should reduce the volume of Mexico-to-US migration when viewed over two or three decades but that NAFTA is likely to increase migration in the 1990s. This increased migration should not become an excuse to slow implementation of NAFTA, since this would also slow the development needed to eventually make migration unnecessary.

Chapter 9 summarizes the policy options for the United States to deal with the NAFTA migration hump. They include encouraging Mexico to cooperate to reduce illegal immigration and dealing with the consequences of increased immigration in the United States.

2

NAFTA, Labor, and Migration

A North American Free Trade Agreement (NAFTA) would create the world's largest free trade area. The NAFTA area's 1992 population of 370 million and its GNP of $6.5 trillion (table 2) equals or exceeds the combined European Community and European Free Trade Association (EFTA) population of 360 million and GNP of $6 trillion. The United States dominates the NAFTA area, accounting for over 85 percent of its GNP, while the major economy in the European Community—Germany—accounts for 25 percent of the European economy.

Canada and the United States have similar GNPs per capita, and they had similar GNP and population growth rates during the 1980s. In both countries, real GNP grew at an annual rate of just over 3 percent, and real GNP per capita grew about 1 percent more slowly because the population rose about 1 percent annually. Furthermore, Canada and the United States have had a free trade agreement since 1989.

Mexico is different. Its GNP increased by only 1 percent annually during the 1980s, and because its population rose 2 percent annually, Mexican GNP per capita fell about 1 percent per year. Although Mexico's economic growth rate has recently been higher than those of the United States and Canada, the economic gaps between Mexico and its two prospective free trading partners widened during the 1980s.

The widening economic gap between Mexico and the United States during the 1980s laid the groundwork for NAFTA. Mexico's President Carlos Salinas de Gortari took office on 1 December 1988, and he soon made major changes in the country's economic policies. Salinas sold state-owned companies, including the telephone company, the national

Table 2 Canada, Mexico, and the United States: selected economic indicators, 1991

	GNP (billions of dollars)	Real GNP growth rate (1980–91)	GNP per capita (dollars)	Real per capita growth rate (1980–91)	Population (millions)	Population growth rate (1980–91)
Canada	569	3.1	21,260	2.1	26.8	1.0
Mexico	252	1.5	2,870	−0.5	87.8	2.0
United States	5,686	3.1	22,560	2.1	252.0	0.9
Total	6,507				366.6	

Source: The World Bank Atlas 1992.

airline, and state-owned steel mills. Tax rates were reduced, and tax collection efforts were stepped up. Banks were reprivatized, and Salinas accelerated the opening of the economy that had begun in the mid-1980s.

The goal was to lay the foundation for export-led growth and to attract domestic and foreign investment into Mexico to produce goods to export. There are several versions of the story of how Mexico reversed its economic policies and embraced free trade with the United States as the best way to accelerate development. Most note that President Salinas toured Europe early in 1990 to announce that Mexico would welcome foreign investments. However, European leaders reportedly told Salinas that, with the fall of communism in 1989, their foreign investments would be concentrated in Eastern Europe. The Europeans suggested that Salinas look to the United States, and he did.

In May 1990 Salinas announced his support for a free trade agreement with the United States, and on 21 September 1990 Salinas formally requested negotiations. President Bush notified Congress on 25 September 1990 that the United States intended to negotiate a free trade agreement with Mexico, and on 17–18 May 1991, Congress voted not to deny Bush the authority to negotiate an FTA with Mexico. Negotiations began on 12 June 1991.

NAFTA is based on four principles (Grayson 1993, 39):

- the elimination of tariff and nontariff barriers to trade between Canada, Mexico, and the United States;

- equal treatment in each country for all goods and services produced in North America;

- a commitment not to erect new obstacles to trade after NAFTA is signed;

- a commitment to extend to NAFTA partners any special trade preferences any of the three countries makes available to non-NAFTA countries.

According to Grayson (1993, 41), it was relatively easy to reach agreement on reducing tariff and nontariff barriers, on safeguards to deal with import surges, and on land transportation issues, such as the right of US drivers to deliver goods inside Mexico. However, most subjects were relatively difficult to agree on: rules of origin, government procurement, energy, subsidies, financial and insurance services, agriculture, investment, and automobiles. Ease of negotiation and the quality of the agreement reached sometimes vary: Hufbauer and Schott (1993, 10) give the NAFTA agreement on safeguards a grade of C but that on transportation an A. Similarly, they give a low grade of C+ to the difficult-to-negotiate energy agreement but an A grade to the agriculture agreement. Hufbauer and Schott endorse NAFTA with an overall grade of B+.

NAFTA's Labor Market Effects

Some parts of NAFTA seemed hard to negotiate because of fears or expectations of how the agreement's provisions would affect particular industries, workers, and communities. Even though Mexico reduced many of its trade barriers before NAFTA negotiations began, Mexico was the most protectionist of the three countries, and thus NAFTA's free trade and investment provisions should lead to more adjustments in Mexico than in the other two countries.

The major economic effect of NAFTA should be to stimulate the flow of investment, goods, and services across North American borders. Trade reflects each country's comparative advantage: if Mexico can buy US corn for less than corn can be produced in Mexico, then Mexicans will enjoy lower food prices. If Mexicans pay for their corn by exporting more cars, then in Mexico ex-farmers might become autoworkers, while in the United States ex-autoworkers might transport or process corn for Mexico. But job gains and losses due to trade are rarely so symmetric; it is more probable that ex-autoworkers would produce industrial machinery or trucks for Mexico.

Even though there are many speculations about NAFTA's effects on the US labor market generally, as well as on particular industry labor markets, there are few analyses that trace an adjustment path for the subsector industries and geographic areas that NAFTA is expected to affect the most. Instead of projecting, for example, rising US employment in machine tools as Mexico imports them to use in newly built factories, followed by falling US employment 5 to 10 years later when Mexico begins to export such goods, most NAFTA analyses involve before-and-after comparisons of variables such as jobs and wage levels. The models reach these conclusions:

- Mexico is the major economic "winner" in NAFTA, but all three countries will have bigger economies, more jobs, and higher wages because of NAFTA.

- Trade between the three economies will rise, and this will increase the GDP of each country, as firms are forced to compete harder and with costs of production falling as firms produce for a larger market. According to the International Trade Commission, Mexico's real GDP could rise by 0.1 to 11.4 percent because of NAFTA, and US and Canadian GDPs might rise by up to 0.5 percent (*Wall Street Journal*, 3 February 1993, A12).

- All three economies should gain jobs and see wages rise as a result of NAFTA. The ITC projected a 7 percent employment gain due to NAFTA in Mexico and up to 1 percent employment gains for the United States and Canada. Real wages in Mexico might rise 0.7 to 16.2 percent because of NAFTA but less than 0.5 percent in the United States and Canada.

Most government, academic, and industry studies echo the conclusion that a signed NAFTA will benefit all of the North American economies and that Mexico will gain the most. NAFTA will help Mexico to lock in recent market-oriented reforms that have raised real economic growth rates to 3 to 4 percent annually and reduced inflation to less than 10 percent. NAFTA should sustain the influx of foreign capital into Mexico that is needed to reform and upgrade lagging sectors of the Mexican economy, including transportation, finance, and agriculture. Mexico can, in this scenario, run a trade deficit for years or decades financed by foreign investors building up the country's infrastructure and productive capacity, much as the United States did in the late 19th century and South Korea did in the 1960s and 1970s.

US exports to and imports from Mexico have skyrocketed since the mid-1980s. Since 1986, for example, US exports to Mexico have almost quadrupled, while US imports from Mexico have doubled. Today's US trade surplus with Mexico is sustained by foreign investors pouring money into what they hope will be North America's first "tiger"—a reference to the fast-growing export-oriented economies of so-called Asian tigers such as South Korea and more recently, Malaysia and Thailand. Mexico will eventually have to export more to justify these investments. When the investments and factories now being built begin to produce, increased Mexican imports into a growing US economy may displace some US workers but also make alternative jobs easier to find.[1]

Restructuring an industry to adjust to new trade patterns can raise productivity and eventually create more higher wage jobs, but there are inevitably layoffs as farms are consolidated and factories close or automate certain processes. Understanding such adjustment scenarios is crucial for understanding the migration consequences of NAFTA. It is very hard simply to predict employment or wage levels five to eight years

---

1. In a talk delivered to the Summer Seminar at the Center for US-Mexican Studies, University of California–San Diego, 19 July 1993, Albert Fishlow expressed surprise at US opposition to NAFTA because short-run oriented politicians seem to be focusing on US job losses that will not occur for 5 to 10 years rather than on the US jobs gains that can be expected during NAFTA's honeymoon period, when jobs are created in Mexico to build factories financed by US investors and filled with imported machinery. Only after Mexico begins to export goods from these factories in order to repay investors is there a threat to US jobs and, by that time, a growing US and world economy should minimize the need for US labor market adjustments.

hence without NAFTA; it is also very hard to predict the increment to these variables that will be due to NAFTA.

Most of the labor market adjustments expected because of NAFTA will occur in Mexico, but one of the most contentious issues in NAFTA ratification is the likely effect of NAFTA on the number and type of US jobs. Since free trade leads to a larger economy, most studies conclude that NAFTA will create more US jobs—not many more, since the Mexican economy is only as large as the economy of Los Angeles, but the United States should have a net 170,000 more jobs due to NAFTA after five years (Hufbauer and Schott 1993, 14). Other studies reach the similar conclusion that the United States will gain about as many net new jobs over five years due to NAFTA as were created during an average month in the late 1980s.

This projected small net increase in US jobs due to NAFTA should make the agreement a nonevent for the US labor market. But NAFTA-related job losses have become a major issue in the United States, with unions projecting the loss of hundreds of thousands of US jobs.[2] In order to avoid these job losses, some unions oppose NAFTA. Others argue that NAFTA should not be approved until acceptable side agreements that upgrade Mexican labor and environmental standards and thus raise the cost of producing goods in Mexico and discourage investment there are negotiated. Both proponents and opponents of NAFTA agree that there must be a Trade Adjustment Assistance (TAA) program for US workers who lose their jobs because of NAFTA.[3]

President Bush said that US workers would be safeguarded through NAFTA provisions that maintained tariffs on sensitive products for 15 years; through a new US-Mexican consultative Commission on Labor Matters that would help to improve and thus standardize workplace safety standards and by a new worker adjustment program that would make available up to $335 million annually for five years to assist workers displaced by NAFTA, an amount that could be doubled if necessary (Hufbauer and Schott 1993, 26–28). President Clinton went further: the labor side agreement his administration negotiated includes a binational or trinational commission that will monitor labor law enforcement.

Labor standards could affect US and Mexican job and wage changes due to NAFTA by influencing the relative attractiveness of producing

---

2. Unions and union-affiliated research groups have projected net US employment losses of 300,000 to 900,000 over a decade as a result of NAFTA. The most-cited study projects a net loss of 550,000 US jobs (Faux and Lee 1992).

3. Since 1961, the United States has had a TAA program to provide unemployment benefits and training for workers who lost their jobs because of increased imports. TAA was an entitlement until March 1993, when the congressional budget committees voted to make the $697 million per year program discretionary or in need of an annual appropriation after July 1994.

in each country. There are two extreme positions. At one extreme, one country's labor laws could be applied to the other—US unions would, of course, prefer that US labor laws apply in Mexican industries that produce goods for the US market, making job flight there less probable.[4] At the other extreme, national labor laws could apply in each country— the norm in trade negotiations between most industrial countries. Finally, international labor standards such as those developed by the International Labor Organization might be applied. Regardless of the labor standard adopted, there must be a body to consider complaints of violations and to assess penalties.

There has been considerable progress toward dealing with US concerns over job losses, but the AFL-CIO remains perhaps the most vocal US critic of NAFTA. During the Bush administration, unions maintained a steady drumbeat of criticism, arguing that NAFTA will benefit multinational corporations at the expense of both US and Mexican workers. US employers, they argue, will move to Mexico because of NAFTA, or threaten to, putting downward pressure on US workers' wages, while any new jobs created for Mexican workers as a result of NAFTA will be in "sweatshops."[5]

Union leaders cite specific fears of job losses. For example, local union leaders noted that a large airport is being built in Tijuana, near the US-Mexican border. They feared that US airlines were involved in the project or would take advantage of its repair facilities for maintenance of US planes at lower Mexican wages. Similarly, US seamen and maritime unions fear that Mexican ships will eventually acquire the right to move cargo between US ports, displacing them, and that modern dry docks will be built in Mexico to repair US ships with Mexican workers. Perhaps the most imaginative example of NAFTA's threat to US workers was a rumor reported by a janitorial union representative that US cleaning companies were considering using weekend airfare and hotel discounts to fly planeloads of Mexicans to US cities to clean office buildings on weekends.[6]

---

4. Mexico in some instances has more proworker labor laws than the United States; if the higher national standard were applied, labor standards would be racheted up.

5. AFL-CIO leaders have used colorful language to describe the problems they see with NAFTA. The executive assistant to AFL-CIO President Lane Kirkland, Jim Baker, asserted that "NAFTA is not a prescription for economic development in Mexico, it is a guarantee of perpetual poverty," which another unionist explained as follows: "If NAFTA passes, Mexicans will be eating beans and rice, Americans will be flipping burgers and a few folks on Wall Street will be trading on our sweat and blood" (AFL-CIO News, 12 October 1992, 1 and 6).

6. These examples were among those discussed at a March 1992 meeting of local union leaders in Ventura, California.

Union leaders have been less vocal opponents of NAFTA since the November 1992 election of President Clinton. However, the AFL-CIO continues to be a critic of NAFTA: its weekly paper for members has included at least one anti-NAFTA article each issue for the past year. Its current campaign, centered on slogans such as "not this NAFTA" and "fix it or nix it," rests on getting acceptable side agreements on "worker rights and environmental standards and import protection, as well as other necessary changes in the existing draft agreement" ("Labor Gears Up Drive Against Flawed NAFTA," *AFL-CIO News*, 19 April 1993, 2). The AFL-CIO was not satisfied with the side agreements announced in August 1993, and unions as well as presidential candidate Ross Perot remain among the most prominent NAFTA critics.

In the United States, job and wage issues due to NAFTA have received the most attention. The most cited study was conducted by Hufbauer and Schott (1992). It assumed that each $69,000 in increased US exports creates one US job, and each $11,700 of expansion of Mexican exports creates one Mexican job (box 5). Based on projected increases in US and Mexican exports due to freer trade, they initially concluded that the United States would gain 130,000 net new jobs because of the agreement and that Mexico would add 609,000 jobs.[7] US exports to Mexico were projected to rise by $16.7 billion because of NAFTA, and imports from Mexico were projected to increase by $7.7 billion. Increased US exports to Mexico would thus create 242,000 US jobs, while increased US imports from Mexico would eliminate 112,000 US jobs. The result was a projected net US gain of 130,000 jobs due to NAFTA over 10 years (Hufbauer and Schott 1992, 60).

The Hufbauer and Schott study was updated in 1993, and changing sales-to-employment ratios in US export industries reduced the amount of trade necessary to create one US job to $51,000 (Hufbauer and Schott 1993). A $1 billion change in the US trade balance thus creates or destroys 19,600 jobs, so that the same projected trade changes create 325,000 new US jobs by 1995. Rising imports from Mexico eliminate 150,000 US jobs, for a net gain of 175,000 US jobs. NAFTA's effects on US wages are also expected to be very small: on the order of a 10-cent increase after four years of NAFTA for a US worker earning $10 per hour.

NAFTA will likely have more significant effects on Mexican employment and wages. According to the 1990 census of population, Mexico

---

7. The methodology is straightforward. To estimate how many US jobs are created by exports and lost to imports, total sales of export industries are divided by employment in them. In the Hufbauer and Schott study, it was determined that each $1 billion in additional US exports creates 14,500 US jobs—that is, each $69,000 change in the trade balance adds or subtracts one US job (Hufbauer and Schott 1992, 58). There is no real basis for estimating US job losses due to imports, but most studies make gains and losses symmetric by assuming that the same sales-to-employment ratio applies, so that, each $1 billion in additional US imports displaces 14,500 US workers.

had a labor force of 24 million. Almost 4.5 million Mexican workers were employed in the manufacturing sector of the economy, which offered 19 million nonfarm jobs in 1989. Manufacturing employment grew rapidly during the 1980s, and one model projected an additional 1.5 million manufacturing jobs in Mexico during the 1990s because of NAFTA. However, other models project no net increase in Mexican employment because of NAFTA, and a few even expect job losses. Hufbauer and Schott, by contrast, projected a 609,000 gain in Mexican employment because of NAFTA. As with US job gains, most studies suggest that NAFTA will help to create jobs in Mexico, but that the trade agreement solves only part of Mexico's need to create 1 million jobs annually for new labor force entrants.

NAFTA is expected to have more effects on Mexican than US wages. Mexican labor costs of $1.20 hourly are projected to rise anywhere from 0 to 16 percent because of the agreement during its first five years, with most estimates in the 2 to 3 percent range. Since Mexico is starting from lower employment and wage bases, the changes in the Mexican labor market due to NAFTA should be more visible to the average Mexican than to the American worker.

Why is the rhetoric so heated when it appears that there will be small but positive effects of NAFTA on jobs and wages in both countries? The answer is based on several trends and fears:

- US private-sector unions have been under pressure throughout the 1980s—jobs were lost, and wage increases were small;

- With NAFTA, unions fear that 1980s conditions will continue—more job losses, downward pressure on wages, and few prospects that union workers who are now laid off will be recalled to their high-wage factory jobs.

- NAFTA is likely to increase foreign investment in Mexican maquiladora-style factories, which US unions have accused of stealing US jobs for 25 years.

American unions would like the wages of Mexican workers employed in export industries to be raised significantly and to deny free access to the US market to products produced in "runaway" US plants in Mexico. The counterargument is that NAFTA will aggravate the eroding position of unionized US manufacturing workers only marginally. NAFTA proponents argue that manufacturing jobs are already leaving the United States, and it is better for jobs that must leave to move to nearby Mexico than to faraway Asia. Mexicans spend a high fraction of additional earnings on imports from the United States, so a NAFTA that causes incomes

Box 5 NAFTA's expected effects on the United States and Mexico

Mexican exports and imports. Mexico exported goods and services worth $33 billion in 1989; three-fourths of Mexico's exports go to the United States. World Bank studies suggest that, in the first years after economic policy liberalization, a country's exports rise at an average real growth rate of 11 percent yearly, which would make Mexico's exports in 1995 in the $62 billion to $68 billion range. Without a NAFTA, Mexico's exports would rise, but at an 8 percent annual rate, to the $52 billion to $58 billion range.

Mexico imported goods and services worth $31 billion in 1989, including US goods worth $300 per capita. Mexico is expected to import as much as its exports and capital imports allow. This means that exports of $65 billion in 1995, plus worker remittances of $4 billion, plus net capital inflows of $10 billion to $12 billion, would permit Mexico to import goods and services worth $80 billion in 1995. Since 70 percent of Mexico's imports are from the United States, a NAFTA that permitted Mexico to import about $80 billion worth of goods in 1995, instead of the $65 billion expected without NAFTA, would boost US exports to Mexico by $15 billion.

Mexico sells three-fourths of its exports to the United States and buys three-fourths of its imports from the United States, so for each $10 billion by which NAFTA increases Mexico's exports, Mexico buys an additional $7.5 billion of US imports by 1995. If Mexico imports an additional $25 billion because of NAFTA in 1995, and if the United States maintains its share of Mexican imports, then there would be an additional $19 billion in US exports. The US trade balance, in this scenario, would improve by about $11.5 billion.

US jobs and wages. In the mid-1980s, each $1 billion net improvement in the US trade balance added about 14,500 US jobs, or every net increase of $70,000 of exports over imports created one US job, and an $11.5 billion increase in the US trade balance by 1995 suggests that an additional 168,000 jobs may be created in the United States by NAFTA. A July 1992 revision in the US export industries sales-to-employment ratio reduced to $51,000 the increase in exports needed to create one US job, so the same trade projections increase the job gain and loss estimates: plus 325,000 new US jobs by 1995,

to rise in nearby Mexico will increase US exports more than would occur if the US jobs had gone to Asia.

NAFTA's Migration Effects

To sum up the preceding section, NAFTA is expected to have small and positive effects on US jobs and wages, and large and positive effects on Mexican jobs and wages. But the major economic relationship between the United States and Mexico has been the binational labor market created when Mexican workers find US jobs. The number of Mexican migrants dwarfs even fairly high estimates of job gains in Mexico due to NAFTA, such as the 60,000 Mexican jobs per year that Hufbauer and Schott expect to be created as a result of NAFTA (1992, 57).

minus 150,000 US jobs due to increased imports from Mexico, for a net US gain of 175,000 jobs. Since the US economy sometimes adds this many jobs in one month, most analyses assume that there will be no effect of NAFTA on overall US wages.

Mexican jobs and wages. Since Mexican manufacturing wages were roughly one-sixth of US manufacturing wages in 1989, it is assumed that a $1 billion increase in Mexico's net exports creates six times more jobs there than in the United States, or 87,000 jobs—that is, job creation costs $11,700 per job in Mexico. With a NAFTA, the Mexican trade balance in goods is expected to improve by $7 billion, creating 609,000 jobs in Mexico by 1995 and adding 2 percent to projected Mexican employment of 30.5 million. Mexican wages may not rise because of persistent un- and underemployment, but the foreign direct investment in Mexico and the return of Mexican flight capital is expected to cause the real peso exchange rate to rise by 30 percent, and if each 1 percent appreciation in the peso reduces Mexican living costs by 0.3 percent, real Mexican wages would rise by 9 percent due to the appreciating peso.

Evaluation. An improvement in the US trade balance of $8 billion to $12 billion and the 115,000 to 175,000 additional US jobs that might be created are almost insignificant in a US economy that exports goods and services worth almost $500 billion annually and imports almost $600 billion annually. However, a net improvement of $7 billion to $8 billion in Mexico's trade balance is very significant in an economy where exports are worth $33 billion and imports $31 billion.

All models agree that the effect of NAFTA on US job creation and US wages will be small—all project a net change in US jobs due to NAFTA after 5 to 10 years that is less than the 200,000 net new jobs added in the US labor market each month during the late 1980s. Most report US wage gains due to NAFTA of 1 or 2 percent, meaning that a $10 per hour wage would rise by 10 or 20 cents by 1995.

Source: Adapted from Hufbauer and Schott (1992, 47–64; 1993).

Of the three major types of Mexico-to-US migrants—legal immigrants, nonimmigrants, and unauthorized migrants—NAFTA references only the least important: nonimmigrants. It does not affect the legal US immigration system. The few migration provisions in NAFTA are similar to those of the Canada–US Free Trade Agreement of 1988: they permit four categories of "business persons" to enter the United States, Canada, and Mexico on a reciprocal basis,[8] but they limit the number of Mexican

---

8. These four categories are business visitors, who enter the United States on B-1 visas, traders (E-1) and investors (E-2), intracompany transferees (L visas), and certain professionals. Only the B-1 and L visas are currently available to Mexicans. The provision of NAFTA dealing with freedom of movement for professionals is borrowed from the Canada–US FTA. These so-called TC professionals must satisfy education or credential requirements, and US employers must certify that the professional alien they seek to employ has these qualifications and that the US job to be filled requires such qualifications.

professionals allowed to work temporarily in the United States to 5,500 annually.

NAFTA also does not include provisions that deal with the unauthorized entry of 1.5 million to 2 million Mexicans annually, including 150,000 to 200,000 who are believed to settle every year in the United States.[9] Instead of requiring Mexico to cooperate with US immigration control efforts,[10] NAFTA is supposed to indirectly reduce such migration.

For most of the 20th century, more Mexicans have migrated to the United States illegally than legally. The United States can affect both the total number of Mexican immigrants and the shares who are immigrants, nonimmigrants, and unauthorized by adjusting its immigration and enforcement policies. In 1954, for example, the United States apprehended over 1 million illegal Mexicans, and by simultaneously doubling nonimmigrant Bracero program admissions to almost 450,000 in 1956, apprehensions were reduced to less than 90,000.

The United States admits relatively few nonimmigrant Mexican workers; Mexicans were 9 percent of the 160,000 temporary workers and trainees admitted in fiscal 1991. In that year, Jamaica sent more nonimmigrant workers (14,600) to the United States than did Mexico (14,000) (US Immigration and Naturalization Service, *Statistical Yearbook* 1991, 101). Mexico supplied less than one-third of the 18,500 nonimmigrant agricultural workers admitted in fiscal 1991, the avenue through which Mexican workers entered the US labor market legally in the past.

The total number of Mexicans who annually enter US labor markets is probably 20 times larger than the 15,000 legal nonimmigrant entries. Some of these Mexicans enter the United States legally as relatives of US citizens and Mexican immigrants who have settled here, and a few enter as needed workers. However, most enter illegally, and many later have their status legalized. About 1.2 million Mexicans were legalized in 1987–88 through a program that granted legal status to those who had been in the United States since 1982, and 900,000 were legalized for

---

9. There is no precise measure of the annual influx or settlement of Mexican immigrants. Espenshade (1991) estimates the annual gross inflow of unauthorized Mexicans at 2 million annually, with 10 percent settling in the United States. A GAO panel in February 1992 concluded that the gross inflow of illegal aliens from all countries was about 2 million annually, three-quarters of whom come from Mexico, and that 10 percent of both types settle in the United States.

10. There are a number of cooperative steps that might have been negotiated. Mexico's constitution prohibits government interference with emigration, but the constitution could be amended, as it has been over 400 times in the past 80 years. Second, Mexican authorities could cooperate to make it more difficult for Mexicans to illegally enter the United States. In a few places, dirt has been used to construct a ramp on the Mexican side of the 12-foot fence at the Tijuana–San Diego border that actually makes it easier for Mexicans to cross. Third, Mexican authorities could do far more to prevent the massing of Mexicans who are waiting to attempt illegal entry into the United States.

having worked at least 90 days in US agriculture in 1985–86. About three-fourths of the first group were in the US labor force (900,000), and all of the second group should have been in the US work force, suggesting that at least 1.8 million Mexicans were illegally employed in the United States in the mid-1980s. This is a stock, not an annual flow, but the widely suggested estimate that the stock of illegal Mexican workers grows by 10 percent annually would suggest that 180,000 unauthorized Mexican workers arrived annually during the 1980s. Usual legal admissions from Mexico add another 20,000 to 30,000 Mexican workers per year to the US labor force.

How will NAFTA affect the net annual addition of at least 200,000 Mexican workers to the US work force? Just as with the projections of the effects of the agreement on jobs and wages, there are a variety of models and methodologies. All agree that there will be substantial Mexico-to-US migration in the 1990s; none suggest that NAFTA will eliminate illegal migration anytime soon. Indeed, most of the migration models that consider NAFTA expect the agreement to increase the flow of Mexicans to the United States. Some of these workers will arrive legally, as those legalized in 1987–88 petition for the entry of family members, and some will come illegally. Since the United States can influence migration status with its immigration and enforcement policies, both legal and illegal flows should be considered when projecting the effects of NAFTA on migration.

The most widely cited projection of NAFTA's effects on Mexico-to-US migration is that of Hinojosa and Robinson (1991). Using a model of the US and Mexican economies and labor markets and then projecting how free trade might affect Mexican agriculture in particular, their model estimated that NAFTA would displace about 1.4 million rural Mexicans, largely due to changes in Mexican farm policies and freer trade in agricultural products. If jobs are not created for these displaced farmers where they live, they are expected to migrate: Hinojosa and Robinson projected that 800,000 would stay in Mexico and that 600,000 would migrate (illegally) to the United States. These 600,000 additional US-bound migrants—say, 100,000 per year over six years—are presumably NAFTA-caused additions to the "normal" flow of legal and illegal Mexican worker arrivals.

Projecting the incremental Mexico-to-US migration is difficult, and the projections summarized in table 1 mix together legal and illegal migration, gross and net migration flows, workers and dependents, migration due to NAFTA versus migration due to other factors, and different periods. All suggest substantial Mexico-to-US migration in the 1990s.

The demographic models come closest to establishing a baseline level of migration. Garcia y Griego (1989) estimated the probability that different genders and age groups of Mexicans migrated to the United States in the 1980s. If these emigration probabilities remain constant in the 1990s, then he projects 40,000 to 100,000 Mexican immigrants annually during the decade. The World Bank uses similar reasoning, but it projects 150,000 to 180,000 Mexican immigrants annually. Both of these models assume that the forces encouraging emigration in the 1980s will remain constant in the 1990s—that is, the dynamic element of the annual migration flow is the number of people in each age and gender category and their past probability of migrating to the United States, not land reform or NAFTA.

Espenshade (1991) developed estimates of unauthorized Mexican migration based on apprehensions. The key assumption is that the probability of a Mexican's being apprehended attempting illegal entry is 30 percent—suggesting that on 7 of 10 occasions an alien eludes the US Border Patrol—so that the relationship between the undocumented flow and the number of apprehensions is 0.3/0.7. Multiplying this ratio times the undocumented flow yields the number of apprehensions.[11] Since apprehensions are known, the estimated undocumented flow is apprehensions times 7/3, or 2.33 (Acevedo and Espenshade 1992, 739). Apprehensions in 1991 and 1992 were about 1.2 million annually, suggesting that there were 2.8 million gross or one-way illegal entries in those years.

The baseline level of illegal immigration—the flow in 1987–88—was estimated to be 2 million annually.[12] At that time, the US unemployment rate for men was 1.6 times the Mexican rate, and US wages were 7.2 times Mexican wages (Acevedo and Espenshade 1992, 737). Espenshade then asked what would happen to the estimated flow of illegal Mexican immigrants if the wage and unemployment gap narrowed. For example, if the Mexican unemployment rate fell 30 percent relative to the US rate, Espenshade estimated that unauthorized Mexican entries would fall by almost 10 percent to 1.8 million annually.[13] A 50 percent fall in the unemployment rate would reduce entries by 20 percent to 1.6 million

---

11. Espenshade (1991) also developed a model that predicted gross unauthorized migration on the basis of Mexico's 15- to 34-year-old population, seasonal agricultural worker applications, US-Mexico wage and unemployment ratios, and enforcement and seasonality variables. This model lays the basis for the relationship between apprehensions and the undocumented flow between 1986 and 1988.

12. The apprehension–gross flow relationship gives approximate results. In 1987 and 1988 there were 1.1 million and 1 million apprehensions, respectively. Applying the 7/3 ratio to them would produce estimated undocumented inflows of 2.3 million to 2.6 million, versus a post-IRCA flow reported to be 2.1 million (Acevedo and Espenshade 1992, 736).

13. This model may not fully capture rural Mexican and rural US variables. For example, the Mexican unemployment rate used—3 to 4 percent in 1987–88—reflects that of urban workers in the largest cities who were separated from formal employment relationships, even though only 35 to 40 percent of the Mexican work force has such employment relationships. The US unemployment rate does not accurately reflect conditions in seasonal agriculture, where many illegal Mexican workers find their first jobs (Mines et al. 1991).

(Acevedo and Espenshade 1992, 738). Similarly, if Mexican wages were to rise by 25 percent relative to US wages, unauthorized migration would fall by 10 percent to 1.8 million. Doubling Mexican wages relative to US wages would decrease apprehensions by 25 percent to 1.5 million. Finally, decreasing relative Mexican unemployment by 30 percent and increasing relative Mexican wages by 25 percent would decrease the influx 20 percent to 1.65 million annually.

These demographic and labor market models project continued and possibly rising Mexico-to-US migration in the 1990s, but they do not isolate NAFTA's effects on particular US and Mexican industries, which in turn might affect migration patterns. Computable general equilibrium (CGE) models, by contrast, seek to describe the process through which inputs such as labor and capital are transformed into goods, some of which are exported, so that when NAFTA changes the ease with which Mexico, for example, can export goods, the effects of these changes on Mexican jobs, wages, and incentives to emigrate can be traced. These models make a number of simplifying assumptions, in some instances assuming full employment in each country, wages that reflect the value of marginal contributions to production rather than minimum or negotiated levels, and no government or speculative influences on the peso-dollar exchange rate.

The Hinojosa-McCleery (1992) CGE model is typical. The model assumes that there were 2.5 million undocumented Mexicans in the United States in 1982 (80 percent of whom were in the US labor force), that the 1982 cost of migrating illegally to the United States, including lost wages, was $1,200, that illegal Mexican workers had $1,200 less net earnings than US workers in the same job, and that Mexicans expect a $3,000 earnings premium[14] when they migrate to the United States (1992, 148–49). According to a "status-quo" simulation, if there had been no Mexican debt crisis, if oil prices had returned to their 1982 levels, and if the United States did not adopt the Immigration Reform and Control Act of 1986, then the stock of unauthorized Mexican immigrants in the United States would have been about 4.6 million in 1990, peaked at 6.6 million in 2000, and then begun to decrease as the Mexican demand for unskilled labor grew enough to absorb more potential US-bound migrants.

The Hinojosa-McCleery model terms what in fact happened during the 1980s the "neoliberal scenario." Mexico began to pay off its foreign debt, the United States attempted to curb illegal immigration, and trade barriers fell in anticipation of a free trade agreement. According to Hinojosa and McCleery (1992, 134), this will result in an average stock of 4.6

---

14. For rural workers averaging $600 to $1,000 per year in Mexico in 1982, this implies US earnings of $3,600 to $4,000 to induce emigration.

million unauthorized Mexican migrants in the United States in the 1990s. They consider this scenario to be unstable because restricting the emigration escape valve for Mexicans drives "wages to the poor in Mexico below the subsistence level by the workings of the enforced free market." At the other extreme, their protectionism scenario imagines effective US controls that stop illegal immigration so that there are no unauthorized Mexican workers in the United States; Mexico defaulting on its foreign debt, ending capital flows to Mexico; and little trade. Once again, this scenario hurts Mexican workers: "Wages for the poor in Mexico are collapsed by the return of deported migrants, again falling below subsistence levels" (Hinojosa and McCleery 1992, 135).

The scenario preferred by Hinojosa and McCleery is "managed interdependence," which seeks to reduce immigration to protect unskilled US workers and to promote investment in Mexico. This "plus-plus" scenario leaves an average 3.9 million unauthorized Mexican migrants in the United States and leads to the largest wage gains for unskilled workers in the two countries.[15]

Levy and van Wijnbergen (1992) developed a CGE model of the Mexican economy that simulated the effects of agricultural policy changes on employment in Mexican agriculture. Their model begins with the costs and benefits of the price supports for maize (corn) and beans that raise the prices Mexican farmers receive for these crops above world prices, and then looks at subsidies provided by the government that reduce consumer prices to below world levels. They assume that Mexicans will stay in rural areas so long as the current 1-to-3 rural-urban income gap does not increase.

Beginning with 6 million employed in Mexican agriculture, including 1.7 million employed to produce corn, Levy and van Wijnbergen project the displacement and migration of 40 percent of the corn farmers and workers if trade is liberalized. These 700,000 workers are displaced in one year in one version of the model to generate the largest gains in

---

15. There are a number of assumptions in the "managed interdependence" scenario whose implications are unclear. For example, managed interdependence includes a "capital transfer scheme" in which $5 billion of US investment per year is matched with new Mexican investment, and the proceeds are shared such that "each group benefits equally from the different values of the marginal product of capital in the two countries." There is also a "migration tax," which "combines normalization of the undocumented migrant's status with taxation of the benefits of normalization—the money raised by the tax is divided between the two countries. The US share is spent on income transfers to compensate those adversely affected by immigration. In Mexico, tax revenues . . . serve to create more high wage jobs and to raise wages for Mexico's low wage workers, thus producing the incentives to migrate" (Hinojosa and McCleery 1992, 136–37). If the 2 million Mexicans legalized in 1987–88 had each paid $2,000 to become legal immigrants, $4 billion would have been raised. However, there were complaints that the $185 legalization fee charged was too high.

economic efficiency. Alternatively, displacement can be held to about 200,000 workers annually (with four dependents each, or 800,000 people) by slowing farm trade liberalization.[16] During the 1990s, Levy and van Wijnbergen project a total 1.9 million displaced workers with complete trade liberalization and 1.2 million without trade liberalization, emphasizing that non-NAFTA factors account for two-thirds of the labor displacement they project in rural Mexico. Even without NAFTA, Levy and van Wijnbergen expect up to 5 million Mexicans to leave the land.

Robinson et al. (1991) follow the Levy approach of separating agriculture into three sectors: corn, fruits and vegetables, and other crops. Like the Levy model, the Robinson et al. model suggests a trade-off between economic efficiency and migration: the faster agricultural trade is liberalized, the greater the economic efficiency gains, but quick liberalization also produces more migration. If agricultural trade is completely liberalized, they project the displacement of 1.4 million rural Mexican workers, and they expect about 43 percent of them to migrate to the United States. These 600,000 displaced Mexican farmers and farm workers could be absorbed in Mexico, they argue, if capital investment pours into Mexico such that economic growth is about 2.5 percent faster there than in the United States. But even sustained growth of 3 percent in the United States and 5.5 percent in Mexico may not eliminate a migration hump due to free trade, since trade liberalization releases farm labor quickly, while it takes time for capital inflows to create jobs and spur growth.

Models that attempt to trace the effects of free trade on migration have been extended to the state level by Hinojosa, Robinson, and Wolff (1991). This model produces similar conclusions: free trade will produce a migration hump that can partially be offset by slowing trade liberalization and stepping up investment in Mexico. This state-level CGE model also asked whether the migration hump is a benefit or burden for California. The migration hump due to free trade, they argued, primarily adds to the supply of workers in segmented US labor markets already dominated by Hispanics so that immigrants already here bear the brunt of any wage depression and unemployment caused by the new arrivals. However, Hinojosa, Robinson, and Wolff assumed no negative fiscal impacts of legal or unauthorized Mexican immigration, an assumption challenged by Muller and Espenshade (1985, 140–41), who found that in 1980, households headed by Mexican immigrants cost Los Angeles County an average of $466 more per household than they paid in taxes. Second, Briggs (1992) has argued that the indirect cost immigration imposed by segmenting US labor markets and leaving an American underclass on welfare should not be ignored.

---

16. A one worker–four dependents ratio means that rural Mexico has 6 million workers and 24 million nonworking dependents, or a population of 30 million.

There are other projections of Mexico-to-US migration that might be categorized as "educated guesses." Their starting point is that Mexico has a high fraction of its work force in agriculture and that this percentage is likely to decrease with free trade and industrialization. The questions are how much, how fast, and where do displaced farm workers go.

Calva (1992) predicts that Mexican agricultural reforms and free trade will displace 15 million people from Mexican agriculture during the 1990s. The reasons for this expected displacement of labor from agriculture include reduced government subsidies (in mid-1993, the Mexican government guaranteed corn farmers 2.15 times the world price), the first-time opportunity to sell or rent communal *ejido* land, and an expected flood of cheaper imported farm products. Although the displacement number may seem large at first blush, it should be noted that Calva's number includes workers and their dependents at a ratio of four dependents per worker. This implies that 3 million of the 6 million currently employed in Mexican agriculture would be displaced, or 300,000 per year.

Luis Tellez, the undersecretary for planning in Mexico's Ministry of Agriculture and Hydraulic Resources, frequently reminds audiences that 27 percent of the Mexican population depends on agriculture, but this sector generates only 9 percent of GDP.[17] The resulting 1-to-3 or 1-to-4 rural-to-urban income gap encourages rural-to-urban and rural-to-US migration. Since there is little prospect that Mexican economic policies or NAFTA will improve rural incomes, the benefits of rapid Mexican economic growth will show up in urban areas, speeding up the rural exodus.

Tellez has suggested on several occasions that Mexico's rural population might shrink by 1 million annually, that up to 15 million rural Mexicans may migrate "within a decade or two" ("The Dream of Land Dies Hard in Mexico," *New York Times*, 27 November 1991, A1). Tellez converted this to a labor displacement figure in May 1992, when he predicted that over 1.4 million farmers and workers would be displaced by 2002 due to freer trade and land reforms.[18]

Tellez did not speculate on where these displaced workers would migrate, but 1988 presidential candidate Cuauhtemoc Cardenas (speech to the World Affairs Council, San Francisco, February 1992) suggested that half may migrate to the United States. He speculated that 2 million

---

17. In 1990 the World Bank reported that Mexico had 86.2 million people and a GDP of $238 billion, for a per capita GDP of $2,490. However, the 23 million rural Mexicans must divide $21 billion among themselves, giving them an average per capita GDP of less than $1,000, while the 63 million urban Mexicans divide $217 billion, giving them an average per capita GDP of $3,400 (World Bank, *World Development Report* 1992, 222–23).

18. Tellez projected that the farm work force would fall from 26 percent in 1992 (7.18 million of 30 million) to 16 percent by 2002 (6.4 million of 40 million). Cited in Cornelius (1992, 6).

families, or 10 million people, would leave Mexico's rural areas during the 1990s, and that of half of these—1 million annual exits—perhaps 100,000 workers would wind up in the US labor market. This is fewer than projected by the CGE models.

Demographic and CGE models as well as educated guesses reach a common conclusion: large-scale Mexico-to-US migration will continue in the 1990s. Furthermore, because of Mexican economic reforms and NAFTA, there is likely to be a migration hump. Acevedo and Espenshade's (1992, 740) conclusion is typical: "In the short-to-medium term, the NAFTA is likely to increase pressures for undocumented migration from Mexico to the United States." Hinojosa and McCleery (1992, 139) echo this point: "An FTA by itself is not capable of reducing migration as some have claimed. Migration, in fact, will increase substantially in the absence of significant capital inflows to increase employment and wages in Mexico."

Most of these projections of a migration hump were made on the basis of aggregate models or the likely effects of national policies. None followed Espenshade's advice (1992, 741): "Future studies of the impact of NAFTA on Mexico-US migration should examine not only the sectors of the American economy that employ Mexican workers but also the corresponding sending regions in Mexico." The next chapter takes up this challenge.

II

NAFTA, Agriculture, and Maquiladoras

3

The Roots of Mexican Migration to the United States

Mexican migration to the United States has its roots in development patterns on both sides of the border that have evolved over the past century. The southwestern US economy developed an enormous appetite for unskilled workers willing to work for low wages. Many of these workers were needed only seasonally, and farms, railroads, and mines became dependent on recently arrived immigrants who were willing to accept intermittent employment. Business decisions were made under the assumption that immigrant workers would be available when they were needed—and paid the minimum wage for that time. This helps explain why US employers for decades resisted restrictions on Mexican immigration.[1]

Mexico neglected the handful of states whose residents were dependent on US earnings, creating a binational labor market. The Mexican workers who participated were sometimes legal immigrants, sometimes nonimmigrant guests, and often unauthorized workers, who were more or less tolerated. Farm employers often talked of obtaining Mexican workers in the same way that they obtained water: open the tap when they are needed, and close it when they are not. One researcher (Fogel 1977, 246) believes this attitude also accurately describes US policy: "The

---

1. Varden Fuller (1991, 7) argued that the structure of California agriculture—its system of large farms dependent on seasonal workers—developed because (immigrant) workers without other US job options were usually available. In his words, the assumption was "that with no particular effort on the part of the employer, a farm labor force would emerge when needed, do its work, and then disappear—accepting the terms and conditions offered, without question."

de facto policy has been—bring them in when they are needed; send them back when they aren't."

The United States set Mexican migration in motion in order to largely solve the difficult problem of ensuring a supply of seasonal farm workers. There have been three major US responses to this perennial problem: diversified family farms, slavery, and hired workers without other US job options. In most of the United States, diversified family farms relied on large families to help out during busy periods; during lulls, farm families had more leisure time. In the South, plantations were so big that even large families could not handle peak-season labor needs, and since warmer weather extended the growing season, slavery was economical. In the West, large farms turned to workers without other job options.

Recently arrived immigrants have been the major source of seasonal farm workers in the West, and the justification for them was developed a century ago. An 1883 editorial in the *Pacific Rural Press* neatly captures the argument: "the (fruit) crop of the present year, although deemed a short one, taxed the labor capacity of the state . . . the labor is not now in the country to handle an increase in production." Since California farmers cannot hope to employ Americans or European immigrants because farmers "cannot employ them profitably . . . more than 3 or 4 months in the year—a condition of things entirely unsuited to the demands of the European laborer," another source of labor had to be found. Asian and Mexican immigrants fit the bill, the argument went, because "crouching and bending (farm) operations must be performed in climatic conditions in which only the Orientals and the Mexicans are adapted" (quoted in Fuller 1942, 19813 and 19868).

These arguments may have a racist tone, but they also captured an important economic justification for the southwestern economy's reliance on immigrant workers. Seasonal workers who were paid only when they were needed were cheaper than year-round hired hands: a California farm spokesman in 1872 observed that hiring Chinese immigrants who housed themselves and then "melted away" when they were not needed made them "more efficient than Negro labor in the South [because] it [Chinese labor] is only employed when actually needed, and is, therefore, less expensive" than slavery (quoted in Fuller 1942, 19809).[2] Second, the subsidy implicit in low farm wages was soon reflected in

---

2. The merits of slavery versus employing seasonal farm workers were debated extensively, with seasonal workers usually found to be cheaper because no capital outlay was required to purchase them; they boarded themselves while employed and reproduced abroad; they were available when needed, but they were paid only for the time they were actually employed; and at the end of the season they "moved on, relieving [the] employer of any burden or responsibility for his [workers'] welfare during the slack season" (Fuller 1942, 19824).

higher land prices, giving farmers an incentive to preserve access to immigrant workers and thus maintain higher land prices. California farmers, for example, tried to have the Chinese Exclusion Act of 1882 repealed, noting that land was worth $200 to $300 per acre in 1888 for fruit production, where the wages paid to Chinese workers were $1.00 to $1.25 per day. Land used to produce grain and hay, by contrast, was worth only $25 to $50 per acre, and the wage paid to white workers on these farms was $2.00 to $3.00 daily (Fuller 1942, 19816).

Development patterns in Mexico contributed to the willingness of Mexicans to emigrate. The seven central states of Mexico—Nuevo Leon, Tamaulipas, Zacatecas, San Luis Potosi, Guanajuato, Jalisco, and Michoacan—contributed over half of all migrants to the United States for most of the 20th century (Cross and Sandos 1981, xvi). During the Mexican Revolution (1913–20), these states became the battleground between the central government in Mexico City and revolutionaries from Mexican states near the US border, and the fighting led most haciendas to reduce employment of permanent and seasonal workers. As a result, many Mexicans left. Between 1910 and 1930, by one estimate, 20 percent of the population left the region. Of these, 1.5 million, or 10 percent of Mexico's entire population, migrated to the United States (Cross and Sandos 1981, 9–10).

US farmers have been vocal advocates for Mexican immigrant workers, and they have succeeded in securing the employment of these workers since World War I. When unions, churches, and other groups complained about the low wages and poor working conditions that prevailed in the US labor markets where immigrant Mexicans found jobs, farmers responded that, while Mexicans may not be desirable as Americans or farming partners, they were necessary to do seasonal farm work. A statement by a Chamber of Commerce spokesperson to Congress in 1926 illustrated common grower sentiments of the time: "We, gentlemen, are just as anxious as you are not to build the civilization of California or any other western district upon a Mexican foundation. We take him because there is nothing else available. We have gone east, west, north, and south, and he is the only man-power available to us" (quoted in Fuller 1942, 19859).

In 1950, farmers testifying before President Truman's Commission on Migratory Labor made a similar argument:

> Cotton is a slave crop, nobody is going to pick it that doesn't have to. The [Mexican] national is about the only reservoir of labor that we know of that really wants to pick cotton . . . people that can get anything else to do, don't want to pick cotton (quoted in President's Commission on Migratory Labor 1951, 20).

In 1990 a representative of the North Carolina Tobacco Growers Association asserted that "two things that made this country great were hard work and tobacco," and then observed that:

> 95 percent of the workers in my area [North Carolina] are Mexican. Wherever you go, they are all you see working. Local workers do not do manual labor

anymore . . .[they] move to other industries, and we're left with bottom-of-
the-barrel workers again. (Jerome Vick testimony before the Commission on
Agricultural Workers, appendix II, 1992, 316)

Many of the Mexicans who came to the United States to find jobs were
seasonal sojourners, not immigrant settlers. According to one estimate,
only about one in three Mexicans who migrated to the United States
between 1910 and 1930 settled here (Garcia y Griego 1981, 4). The sojourner
nature of Mexican immigration was encouraged by the seasonal need for
Mexican labor in the United States and by periodic repatriations. For example, about 200,000 Mexicans settled in the United States during the 1920s,
but between 1929 and 1933 an estimated 400,000 Mexicans were returned
to Mexico. Their forced return discouraged other Mexicans from attempting
to enter the United States during the Depression.

During the 1930s, there was a widespread feeling that Mexican immigration contributed to an oversupply of labor that in turn held down
wages and prevented unions from improving wages and working conditions, especially in farm labor markets. In 1939, these conditions were
memorialized in John Steinbeck's *The Grapes of Wrath*. The US Senate's
LaFollette Committee also held hearings during the late 1930s on how
farmers and other western employers manipulated immigration and local
law enforcement agencies to prevent workers from bargaining for wage
increases.

Reformers hoped that this outpouring of reports critical of these farmers would lead to lasting reforms. Two reform scenarios were proposed.
Some reformers wanted to restructure large farms into family-sized units
in order to eliminate the seasonal demand for labor and the problems
associated with it. Others wanted to give farm workers who labored in
factories-in-the-fields the labor rights that had been granted in the mid-
1930s to nonfarm workers. Large farms paying factory-style wages could
attract American workers, this argument went, making it unnecessary
to import immigrant farm workers.

The Bracero Program

World War II prevented the implementation of suggested farm labor
reforms. In the spring of 1942 farmers predicted that there would be
labor shortages during the fall harvest and asked the US government
to recruit Mexican workers in order to avoid crop losses. Reformers
complained bitterly that there was no shortage of workers: growers' cries
of labor shortages were, they argued, "a mere repetition of the age-old
obsession of all farmers for a surplus labor supply" (quoted in Craig
1971, 38–39), but farmers won the right to import Mexican workers,
known as Braceros, by arguing that crop losses caused by labor shortages
would hamper the war effort.

In August 1942 the US and Mexican governments concluded an agreement to import Braceros to do farm work in the United States when US workers were not available. The Mexican government, sensitive about the conditions under which some of its nationals had previously worked in the United States[3] and doubtful that there was a real labor shortage in US agriculture, insisted that the US government guarantee the contracts that farmers provided to Mexican workers, including round-trip transportation and the payment of wages equal to those of similar American workers (Craig 1971, 41). The US government admitted these workers by establishing an exception to immigration laws for "native-born residents of North America, South America, and Central America, and the islands adjacent thereto, desiring to perform agricultural labor in the United States." Some 4,000 Braceros arrived in 1942.

The Bracero program brought 5 million rural Mexicans to rural America over the next two decades in an "unprecedented experiment in inter-American labor migration" (Craig 1971, 51). Braceros continued the dependence of US farmers on a work force with no other US job options and institutionalized the dependence of many rural Mexicans on the US labor market. The Bracero program was small during the war years: admissions peaked at 62,000 in 1944, less than 2 percent of the United States' 4 million hired workers. However, Braceros were concentrated on a few farms in a few states where their impacts were significant. They were employed primarily in the southwestern states, the majority in California, and then only on the largest farms. Fewer than 50,000, or 2 percent, of the nation's commercial farms ever employed Braceros. Most Braceros picked cotton during the program's first years.

The Bracero program with the US government as the contractor of Mexican workers lapsed on 31 December 1947, and several years of informal and private US employer recruitment of Mexican workers followed. Illegal immigration increased as Braceros learned they did not have to bribe local Mexican officials to get on recruitment lists and then pay additional bribes at Mexican recruitment centers to work in the United States. US farmers were pleased because they could employ Mexican workers without having their housing for Braceros inspected and being required to offer them the minimum or government-calculated prevailing wage, whichever was higher.

Many Mexicans were legalized after they arrived in the United States, in a process that came to be termed, even in official US government publications, as "drying out the wetbacks" (President's Commission on Migratory Labor 1951). The number of aliens who were legalized after arriving and working illegally far exceeded the number of Mexican work-

3. The Mexican government did not permit Braceros to be employed legally in Texas during the war years because of past abuses.

ers that US employers contracted legally in Mexico. In 1949, for example, about 20,000 Mexicans received contracts from US employers at recruitment centers in Mexico and legally entered the United States as contract workers, while over 87,000 arrived illegally in the United States and then had their status legalized after they found jobs (President's Commission on Migratory Labor 1951, 53).

The President's Commission on Migratory Labor was established in 1951 to determine whether US agriculture needed Mexican immigrants. The commission concluded they were not. It recommended (1951, 178–80) that "no special measures be adopted to increase the number of alien contract workers beyond the number admitted in 1950," which was 67,500. The United States, it argued, could produce food for the Korean War emergency by using its domestic work force more effectively. Furthermore, the commission recommended that "legislation be enacted making it unlawful to employ aliens illegally in the United States" and that "legalization for employment purposes of aliens illegally in the United States be discontinued and forbidden."

These recommendations were not adopted. Growers tied their request for a new Bracero program to the nation's ability to win the Korean War, and in 1951 Congress enacted PL-78, or the Mexican Farm Labor Program (Craig 1971), which is what is usually meant by references to "the" Bracero program.

The PL-78 Bracero program sowed the seeds for contemporary Mexico-to-US migration by permitting US agriculture to expand and creating a demand-pull for Mexican workers. As US workers with the option of seeking nonfarm jobs learned that they did not face Bracero competition in nonfarm labor markets, they abandoned the farm labor market, and the Bracero share of the work force harvesting citrus, tomatoes, and lettuce soon exceeded 50 percent. Farm wages as a percentage of manufacturing wages fell in California during the Bracero-dominated 1950s.[4]

The Bracero program also added to supply-push factors by reinforcing patterns of development in rural Mexico that made millions of Mexicans dependent on the US labor market.[5] Finally, the Bracero program gave million of Mexicans experience in the US job market. Even though most

---

4. In 1950 average California farm wages were $.85 per hour, about 53 percent of the $1.60 average manufacturing wage. In 1960 farm wages averaged $1.20 per hour, only 46 percent of the average manufacturing wage (consumer prices rose 35 percent during the 1950s). Nonfarm workers in the 1950s were also getting fringe benefits such as health insurance for their families and pensions. Such fringe benefits were a rarity for farm workers.

5. Mexico in 1940 launched a Green Revolution to increase agricultural productivity, but the result was two-track agriculture in which the benefits of irrigation, modern seeds and chemicals, and credit accrued primarily to the largest rural landowners. The Green Revolution in Mexico increased rural joblessness and encouraged urbanization and migration.

Table 3   Mexico: Braceros, apprehensions, and immigrants, 1942–64

Year	Braceros	Apprehensions	Immigrants
1942	4,203	n.a.	2,378
1943	52,098	8,189	4,172
1944	62,170	26,689	6,598
1945	49,454	63,602	6,702
1946	32,043	91,456	7,146
1947	19,632	182,986	7,558
1948	35,345	179,385	8,384
1949	107,000	278,538	8,803
1950	67,500	458,215	6,744
1951	192,000	500,000	6,153
1952	197,100	543,538	9,079
1953	201,380	865,318	17,183
1954	309,033	1,075,168	30,645
1955	398,650	242,608	43,702
1956	445,197	72,442	61,320
1957	436,049	44,451	49,321
1958	432,857	37,242	26,721
1959	437,643	30,196	22,909
1960	315,846	29,651	32,708
1961	291,420	29,817	41,476
1962	194,978	30,272	55,805
1963	186,865	39,124	55,986
1964	177,736	43,844	34,448
Total	4,646,199	4,872,731	545,941

Source: US Immigration and Naturalization Service, Statistical Yearbook, various years.

Braceros returned to Mexico at the end of the season, they were making contacts that would prove useful to obtaining US jobs after the program was terminated in 1964.

Braceros and Illegal Aliens

There was considerable illegal immigration alongside legal Bracero entries. Between 1942 and 1964 there were 4.6 million Braceros and 4.9 million Mexicans apprehended in the United States (table 3). The Mexican government was concerned during the late 1940s about its nationals going north illegally, and in the negotiations leading up to the PL-78 agreement, "the Mexican government, press, and citizen [sic] . . . contended that the wetback exodus could be stopped only when [US] employers were penalized for hiring them" (Craig 1971, 75). President Truman endorsed Mexico's plea for US employer sanctions, but he could not persuade Congress to go along with penalties on US employers who knowingly hired illegal aliens. Bracero proponents argued that this legal sidedoor would reduce illegal immigration, but the facts proved them wrong. As table 3 shows, during the early 1950s the number of Braceros and illegal immigrants increased together. *Life* magazine published "Wetbacks Swarm In" in 1951. After the US attorney general toured the border area in 1953, the general of the Sixth Army was appointed commissioner of the US Immigration and Naturalization Service in 1954 with instructions to stop illegal immigration.

The INS launched "Operation Wetback" in 1954. State and local law enforcement authorities joined the INS in coordinated sweeps to round up and deport illegal Mexican immigrants (Craig 1971, 128). As these sweeps spread to inland cities such as Kansas City and Chicago, many Mexicans returned home of their own accord. Still, in 1954 almost 1.1 million illegal aliens were apprehended. The Bracero program expanded to accommodate more legal Mexican workers so that the ratio of apprehensions to Braceros was reversed: in 1951–52 there were five apprehensions per Bracero admission; by 1956–57 there were five Bracero admissions per apprehension.

The Bracero program grew during the 1950s and was phased out in the early 1960s unilaterally by the United States. Growers made the familiar arguments for Braceros: American workers were not available, without the immigrants crops would rot and food prices would rise, and the admission of Braceros had no adverse effects on US workers. However, opponents used the civil rights struggle of the early 1960s to argue that the federal government was impeding the upward mobility of Hispanic farm workers by permitting the importation of Mexican workers. The 1960 television documentary "Harvest of Shame" strengthened the push for ending the Bracero program, and President Kennedy was convinced that Braceros were "adversely affecting the wages, working conditions, and employment opportunities of our own agricultural workers . . . the workers most seriously affected are those from underprivileged groups which are already at the bottom of our economic scale." Nevertheless, he reluctantly signed a two-year extension of the program in 1961 (Craig 1971, 172–73), in part because of the "serious impact in Mexico if thousands of workers employed in this country were summarily deprived of this much-needed employment."

By the early 1960s, Braceros were essential for harvesting only a few crops. In 1962, for example, 60 percent of the Braceros in California were employed to pick the cannery tomatoes that were processed into ketchup, and Braceros were over 80 percent of this crop's harvest work force. As cotton and other geographically dispersed crops were mechanized, the Bracero program became a nonimmigrant program for a handful of farmers, and political support in the United States for its continuation weakened. When a mechanical tomato harvester was developed in California in the early 1960s, for example, one-fourth of the Braceros who were being admitted to the United States were no longer needed.

The Mexican government publicly did not oppose an end to the Bracero program. Even though most Mexican statements acknowledged that there would be adjustment costs if Mexicans could no longer work in the United States, stories of the abuse Mexicans had endured in US fields convinced many Mexicans that the program should be ended. Behind the scenes, however, the Mexican government was lobbying for its continuation. In 1963, for example, the Mexican ambassador opposed an end to the Bracero program because of an expected increase in both illegal Mexican immigration and in permanent Mexican migration to the United States,[6] and the loss of jobs and earnings for 200,000 Braceros and their families (Craig 1971, 186–88). According to one scholar, "Mexico was largely responsible for the final extension" of the Bracero program, which was terminated on 31 December 1964.

Foreign workers could still be imported under the H-2 section of the Immigration and Nationality Act of 1952, under which Jamaicans were imported to hand-cut sugarcane in Florida. However, the US secretary of labor published regulations in December 1964 that made it difficult to import Mexican farm workers under the program. Many US senators were outraged, and in a fight reminiscent of those during the Bracero years, tried to transfer authority to certify the need for alien farm workers from the Department of Labor to the Department of Agriculture. They failed in the Senate only because the vice president cast the deciding vote (Congressional Research Service 1980, 42).

The Bracero Program's Legacy

The year 1965 saw a scramble for farm workers. One California farm employer of 2,000 Braceros hired over 8,000 American workers in 1965. The number of migrant farm workers reached a postwar peak of 466,000 in 1965. Grower interest in mechanization was such that a major study predicted that by 1975 if a fruit or vegetable could not be harvested mechanically, it would not be grown in the United States (Cargill and Rossmiller 1970). The federal government launched a series of programs to help farm workers find nonfarm jobs before they could be displaced by machines (Martin and Martin 1993, chapter 2). Finally, in 1965, a community organizer named Cesar Chavez joined a strike called by California grape pickers to obtain a wage increase, eventually settling it with a one-year, 40 percent wage increase because Braceros were not available to break it.

---

6. Some 30,000 Mexican farm workers obtained immigrant visas in 1963 and 40,000 in 1964, beginning the process of substituting green-card immigrants for Braceros (Craig 1971, 187).

US farm workers generally and California farm workers in particular enjoyed a golden era between 1965 and 1980. Farm worker issues were kept alive by grape and lettuce boycotts mounted by the United Farm Workers (UFW) union, and even though most California growers were not affected by union activities, many were willing to pay "union wages" in order to reduce support among their workers for the UFW. For the first time in decades, the ratio of average farm to nonfarm wages rose above 50 percent.

Immigration began to undermine the UFW in the late 1960s. Under US immigration law, there was no quota during the late 1960s on the number of Mexican workers who could become legal US immigrants on the basis of letters from US employers certifying that they had US jobs. Mexicans who secured immigrant visas in this manner got green cards certifying their immigrant status from the INS, and since most of them commuted from homes in Mexico to seasonal jobs in the United States, they were known as green-card commuters. Such immigrants were required to report annually to the INS, and in January 1967 there were 354,000 Mexican green-carders, including an estimated 65,000 farm workers (London and Anderson 1970, 10).

These green-card commuters, many of whom were ex-Braceros, were criticized as strike breakers. In addition, the UFW and farm-worker advocates accused them of depressing US wages; they reportedly were willing to work for lower wages than US citizens because they had low living costs in Mexico. As these green-card farm workers aged, many became foremen and farm labor contractors (FLCs). In this role, they brought younger Mexican workers, usually illegally, to the United States in the 1970s and 1980s.

At first, the UFW could ignore the gradually increasing role of FLCs and illegal aliens. The UFW achieved much of its success at the bargaining table by threatening consumer boycotts and obtaining favorable legislation, not by controlling the supply of labor. However, after the number of aliens apprehended in the United States surpassed 1 million in 1977, the FLC–illegal alien "problem" could no longer be ignored. The UFW supported employer sanctions and a well-funded INS to enforce them.

Illegal immigration combined with the changing structure of agricultural production and internal UFW turmoil to lead to the demise of the union.[7] In what became a familiar story, aging UFW members were willing to call strikes in the early 1980s for higher wages, despite the availability of FLCs and their crews of recently arrived workers. Easily boycotted brand-name companies had by the early 1980s begun to buy their produce from "independent" growers, who in turn were quick to turn to FLCs to break strikes. Changes in the administration of Califor-

---

7. This section is based on my chapter in Voos (1994).

nia's farm labor relations law ended the tendency of the UFW to win legally what it could not accomplish with economic tools, and the UFW spiraled downward in contracts and members: from 120 contracts and 60,000 members in 1980 to 20 contracts and 6,000 members in 1990. There was little animus between displaced union workers and newly arrived illegal workers in agriculture. Many of the new immigrants were friends and relatives of the unionized workers, and the union workers often excused immigrants' willingness to break strikes with the shrug, saying that such workers had to eat too. The UFW and its supporters were aware of such ties, and they blamed the demise of the UFW on the changed administration of the labor relations law, not on illegal immigration: Dolores Huerta, vice president of the UFW, asserted repeatedly that the number of farm workers was not the problem; the problem was that the government did not enforce labor laws.

The Bracero program is widely credited with setting in motion socioeconomic forces that led to the illegal immigration of Mexicans in the 1970s and 1980s. The Bracero program reinforced and expanded patterns of Mexico-to-US migration that took on a life of their own: "For many rural Mexican males, the Bracero program was an eye-opener; they learned about American jobs and wages; many responded to their employers' interests in bypassing the federally regulated program during its existence; and many kept traveling north after the program ended, despite the fact that those trips were illegal ones" (North and Houstoun 1976, 12). Many researchers assert that the United States created its own illegal Mexican alien problem by setting these migration patterns in motion. Most illegal Mexican aliens during the 1970s and 1980s came from the same Mexican states in which Braceros were recruited, leading one researcher to conclude that "the 'illegal alien' problem is therefore one whose seed has been planted time and again by the US when it has been in need of Mexican labor" (Cardenas 1975, 89).

The Bracero program set in motion migration forces that have proved difficult to regulate. In Mexico, it created an expectation that the fastest way to upward mobility was to go north. In the United States, farmers and other employers made investments on the assumption that such workers would always be available under Bracero-type conditions. The Bracero program also had important second-round effects in the United States. Braceros in the fields held down wages there, and a booming nonfarm economy offered higher-wage urban jobs, so Mexican-Americans during the 1950s changed from a predominantly rural to a mostly urban population. The availability of Braceros permitted the southwestern states to become the garden states of the United States.

4

The Demand-Pull in the United States for Mexican Workers

As discussed in the previous chapter, Mexican workers have been available to the southwestern economy of the United States for over 70 years. Consequently, certain US employers, industries, and areas depend on unskilled workers who will accept seasonal, split-shift, night, and weekend jobs that pay the minimum wage or a bit more. Mexican workers fit the bill, and a combination of immigrant, nonimmigrant, and unauthorized entries has produced a binational labor market between the United States and Mexico.

This chapter and the two following describe this binational labor market, emphasizing the roles of rural Mexicans in rural US labor markets. The reason for the agricultural focus is straightforward: the need for farm workers has been used to justify US programs to recruit Mexican workers, and it is in rural Mexico that the dependence on the US labor market is most pronounced. Since rural Mexican–to–rural American networks are best-developed, they are also the best examples of the bridges that now link the two countries' labor markets, often in defiance of US immigration laws.

Why Do Industries Become Dependent on Immigrants?

Most economic theories of migration focus on why individuals move. Individuals, this theory goes, think of migration as an investment that will eventually repay itself; in this way, migration is analogous to acquiring an education, in the sense that costs today are rewarded by higher incomes later. However, it is not enough to know that the US-Mexican wage gap is 8 to 1; a potential migrant also considers the probability of a person with his skills, language abilities, and contacts finding a job. A potential migrant compares *expected* earnings (wages times the probability of getting a job) at home and abroad, and responds in a manner that maximizes expected earnings (Todaro 1969).

This expected earnings theory of migration has been extended from individuals to families or households (Stark 1991). Often large families in rural areas are assumed to determine how each member can contribute to the family's income, reduce the risk that the family will have no income, and raise the family's income relative to its peer group. Although maximizing expected income is still the family's primary goal, this "new economics of migration" theory emphasizes that a farm family's decision to plant a new crop, or its desire for capital to install an irrigation system, may encourage it to send an older son or daughter abroad, so that labor migration is a mechanism to cope with the absence of crop insurance and credit markets. The household focus also helps to explain why migration seems to beget more migration in many villages: friends and relatives abroad can provide information on wages and job possibilities, and the remittances they send home may make families without anyone abroad relatively poorer. Thus, migration abroad may be a family's response to income inequality in its peer group (Taylor 1992).

Theories that focus on why individuals or households participate in labor migration suggest that narrowing wage and unemployment gaps are likely to reduce the number of people migrating. The household risk and relative deprivation addenda introduce additional options to reduce migration: crop insurance, credit markets, and unemployment insurance would make it less necessary for households to send members abroad to cope with these risks, and taxes and subsidies that limited income inequality would reduce migration motivated by jealousy toward a neighbor's remittances.

Economic theories presume that labor migration will eventually be self-stopping, in the sense that the movement that does occur will reduce the expected earnings differences that motivated it. But there are theories to explain how industries or economies become structurally dependent on immigrant workers, maintaining a demand-pull for migrant workers. Piore (1979), for example, argued that industrial economies inevitably have bad or secondary jobs and that the exhaustion of domestic labor reserves creates and maintains a demand-pull for migrants.

Industrial economies have a persisting need for immigrant workers because they can neither eliminate nor make attractive low-level jobs. According to Piore, most people work both to earn wages and to enjoy the status that goes with their jobs; thus, it is hard to motivate "normal" workers at the bottom of the job hierarchy. Those earning supplemental money (students who work in the summer) and migrants who aim for a target level of savings before returning, by contrast, are willing to work hard as dishwashers, hotel maids, and farm workers.

Couldn't low-level jobs be eliminated through mechanization, exporting them, or raising wages? Piore thinks not. Machines must be paid for whether they are in use or idle, and Piore argues that employers who offer seasonal jobs would rather hire easily laid off workers than buy machinery. If bottom-level jobs are eliminated through mechanization or relocating them overseas, there will still be a bottom in the remaining job hierarchy. Wages for such jobs are hard to raise, according to Piore, because they reflect both social expectations as well as labor supply and demand: if wages for dishwashers were raised in response to a labor shortage, then wages for waitresses and bartenders would also have to increase so that these higher-wage employees maintain their position in the wage hierarchy.

Employers unable to raise wages or otherwise motivate workers in low-level jobs first turn to students, housewives, minorities, and internal rural-urban migrants. Eventually these sources of labor are dried up by the structural changes in agriculture, which deplete the pool of workers willing to fill secondary jobs in urban areas, and by civil rights laws, which reduce discriminatory practices that confine them to such jobs. At that point, employers turn to immigrants, creating a demand-pull that governments are unwilling to eliminate because of the nonmarginal changes in economic organization that would be required.

Dual labor-market theories argue that the persistence of low-level jobs in industrial economies creates and maintains a demand-pull for immigrant workers. World systems theorists, by contrast, argue that the evolution of the world economy has made international labor migration necessary (Wallerstein 1974; Portes and Walton 1981; Massey 1989). As markets and trade spread, they disrupt traditional economic and social systems. Emigration is a natural outgrowth of the disruptions and dislocations that accompany the agricultural revolution and the introduction of wage-paying labor markets in the urban areas of developing nations. Peasants stream into urban areas, this argument runs, where they have access to communications and transportation links that can take them abroad as migrant workers. Industrial countries that recruit migrant workers discover that labor migration is far easier to start than stop.

World systems theories suggest that labor migration is a natural counterflow to goods and investment from industrial economies, which disrupt traditional ways of life and create mobile populations. Industrial-country governments concerned today about unwanted immigration are, in this view, merely reaping the consequences of past colonial, labor recruitment, and multinational business policies. Most world systems theories emphasize that industrial countries are responsible for their own migration problems: many argue that industrial-country support and protection for multinational firms lies at the root of subsequent migration. Many are skeptical that industrial-country governments will take effective steps to curb immigration, since migrant workers, in their view, help to discipline the native work force, to keep emigration countries poor by taking from them their best and brightest (the so-called brain and brawn drains), or to hold down the costs of household help and other services elites require.

Regardless of whether individual or household choices, employer recruitment, or spreading markets set the labor migration flows in motion, migration tends to increase. In a process termed "cumulative causation" (Massey et al. 1994), established migrants lower the cost and risk of migration for later arrivals. The supply of migrants wanting to enter soon exceeds the demand, and entrepreneurs emerge to help migrants evade immigration controls. Within industrial countries, advocates for migrant workers emerge to provide them with counseling and, in some cases, sanctuary from immigration authorities. The result is often a culture of emigration in sending areas, the means to turn potential movement into migration, and jobs and shelter for new arrivals in the industrial country.

Migrant worker flows would diminish if jobs for them dried up. But they rarely do. Once an industry or occupation becomes dependent on migrant workers, it is rarely able to revert to natives. When the United States terminated the Bracero program in 1964, most of the jobs filled by Braceros were eliminated through mechanization. In Europe, where guestworkers became significant proportions of mining and manufacturing work forces in the 1960s, declining demand and automation eliminated jobs—native workers were not induced to replace retired and departed migrants despite campaigns in countries such as France to "redignify" manual labor.

There are many explanations for why dependence on migrant workers seems to be a one-way street. Some observers emphasize "social labeling": once a job is considered a migrant job, natives shun it (Böhning 1972). Others point to changes that occur and make it difficult for native workers to learn about "immigrant jobs." Once a migrant network develops to supply a farm or factory with workers, the language of the workplace may change, and job vacancies tend to be filed informally through the network rather than through newspaper ads or employment services. Such a transition has occurred throughout US agriculture: the traditional easy-entry farm worker occupation is today often closed to monolingual English-speaking workers, most of whom have no contacts with the non-English-speaking crew bosses who do most of the hiring.

A Picture of US Agriculture

Agriculture, the traditional port of entry for Mexican immigrants, provides a classic illustration of this industry dependence. Even though US agriculture employs just 2 million to 3 million wage and salary workers at some time during a typical year, over half of the Mexican immigrants in the US labor force had at least one US farm job. Because Mexicans figured so prominently in 1980s immigration, about one-fourth of the total 6 million immigrants who entered the US labor force during the 1980s had at least one farm job.[1] If 1980s immigration patterns continue in the 1990s, up to one-fourth of the working-age US immigrants who arrive during the decade may be Mexicans whose initial US employment is in fruit and vegetable agriculture.

Agriculture is a difficult industry to reform because it is old and well-organized, geographically dispersed, and resistant to change. Farmers typically belong to multiple farm organizations, which all lobby Congress on behalf of what appears to be a significant number of producers. Farming is dispersed throughout the country, so that most political representatives are sensitive to farmers' concerns. Finally, agriculture uniquely resists change because it is considered an American success story, and farmers are considered today's living links to the founding fathers.

The agricultural reality is different from the myths (box 6). A handful of large farms produce most of the nation's food and fiber. The largest 5 percent of all farms, each a significant business, account for over half of the nation's farm output, while the smallest two-thirds of US farms account for 5 percent of all farm output, and they, on average, lose money farming (*Statistical Abstract of the United States*, 1992, 649). Most American farms are family farms—defined by the US Department of Agriculture as those that can operate with less than the equivalent of one and one-half year-round hired hands—and it is these livestock and grain operations that wrote the American agricultural success story. These farms do not figure prominently in the agriculture and migration story, but they figure prominently in arguments that, without Mexican workers, many farmers would be pushed off the land.

Demand-Pull in Fruit and Vegetable Farming

The subsector of US agriculture most closely associated with the US demand-pull for Mexican immigrants is fruit, vegetable, and horticultural specialties (FVH) such as flowers and nursery products, which encom-

---

1. About 600,000 legal immigrants entered the United States annually during the 1980s, and 50 percent, or 300,000, joined the labor force, including about 5 percent (150,000 out of 3 million) who had farming occupations (US Department of Labor 1989, 25 and 27). About 80 percent of the 1.8 million general legalization applicants were in the labor force, including 80,000 farm workers, who were 5 percent of the 1.44 million general legalization applicants in the labor force, and all of the 1.3 million special agricultural worker (SAW) applicants should have done farm work in the mid-1980s. The Immigration and Naturalization Service indicated in mid-1993 that it had approved almost 1.1 million SAW applications.

Box 6 Farming and farm employment

The US Department of Agriculture defines a farm as "any place from which $1,000 or more of agricultural products were produced and sold or normally would have been sold during the census year," that is, the years ending in 2 or 7. According to this definition, there were 2.1 million farms in 1991. About 20 percent of all farms are in Texas, Missouri, and Iowa.

The largest 107,000 farms each sold farm products worth $250,000 or more in 1991, and they accounted for 56 percent of gross cash income. The smallest 1.3 million farms each sold farm products worth $20,000 or less, and they accounted for 5 percent of gross cash income. These small farms lost $500 million.

Farmers had cash marketing receipts of $170 billion in 1990, including 53 percent from the sale of livestock products and 47 percent from crop products. Production expenses were $144 billion, but with government payments and other farm cash income, net farm income was $51 billion.

Exports of farm products in 1990 were $40 billion, or 11 percent of the total $366 billion in US exports. US imports of agricultural products were $23 billion, 5 percent of US imports, leaving a net agricultural trade surplus of $17 billion.

In 1990 US farm exports included $3 billion worth of fruits and nuts (both fresh and processed), and $2 billion worth of vegetables (fresh and processed), up sharply from 1986 levels of $2 billion and $1 billion, respectively. Imports of fruits and nuts (fresh and processed) were worth $2.5 billion in 1990, and imports of vegetables were worth $2.3 billion. Tomatoes (fresh and processed) worth $400 million were the largest vegetable import.

About 4.6 million people lived on farms in 1990. However, most of the 2.5 million farm residents who are in the labor force are not employed in agriculture: 52 percent are employed off the farm. Most farm workers also live in towns and cities; although data are inadequate, it is believed that fewer than 10 percent of US farm workers live on farms.

Source: Statistical Abstract of the United States 1992 and US Department of Agriculture, *Economic Indicators of the Farm Sector*, 1993.

pass 75,000 US farms. The industry accounts for only 10 percent of all US farm employers and 1 percent of total US employers, but no group has been better able to gain access to Mexican immigrant workers.

The real actors in FVH agriculture are the largest 10 percent of these farms. They account for 80 percent of US fruit and vegetable production and employment, often through a bewildering number of partnerships and corporations. It is true that most US farms, as well as most fruit and vegetable operations, are small, family-run operations, but seasonal factories in the fields account for most of US farm worker employment, and it is the decisions of these large enterprises about where to produce that will influence the demand for rural Mexican workers in the United States during the 1990s and beyond.

US fruit, vegetable, and horticultural specialty (FVH) agriculture has rarely lacked access to immigrant workers, and the industry does not expect them to disappear in the 1990s. The major study of NAFTA's likely effects on US fruit and vegetable agriculture, done for the American Farm Bureau Federation, noted that there were as many complaints from Mexican growers of "labor shortages" as from American growers, and the report concluded that large Mexican farmers in 1991 felt that labor was more of an obstacle to expansion than American growers (Cook et al. 1991). A common refrain in Mexico is that the "many of the best workers do migrate and work in the United States where the wages are higher"(Runsten 1992, 1087). This industry view contrasts sharply with the hopes of US negotiations. Former US Trade Representative Carla Hills predicted that 1.6 million potential Mexican immigrants would "forego those lower-skilled jobs in the US and stay at home" if NAFTA were approved. (*New York Times*, 15 August 1992, A20).

During the 1980s, rural Mexicans were drawn into rural America to support the continued expansion of FVH agriculture. They also spread from their traditional base in southwestern agriculture to farm jobs throughout the United States and to nonfarm jobs in the Southwest, and they experienced an apparent acceleration of the revolving door through which Mexicans and other farm workers leave seasonal jobs. FVH commodities can be produced far from the place where they will be consumed, and Mexico has demonstrated its ability to produce tomatoes and other vegetables competitively for the US market. Consequently, the first leg of the three-legged stool of demand-pull, supply-push, and network forces that induce migration is concerned with how NAFTA will affect the demand-pull for Mexican immigrants in US FVH agriculture in the 1990s.

Fruits and vegetables play a small but growing role in US agriculture. Farmers received an average of $21 billion for the fruits and vegetables they sold between 1986 and 1990, or about one-fourth of the $80 billion value of all crops sold.[2] Despite the fact that vegetable receipts are about equal to those for soybeans or corn and fruit sales exceed wheat sales, fruits and vegetables rarely figure prominently in farm policy debates. There are many reasons, including the fact that fruits and vegetables are grown on only 3 percent of US harvested cropland and that federal budget outlays for them are small relative to outlays for other crops.

2. In 1959 the Census of Agriculture reported that the value of US fruit and nut, vegetable and melon, and horticultural specialty (FVH) production was $2.7 billion, or 9 percent of the total $30 billion of US farm sales. By 1980 FVH sales, as estimated by USDA, totaled $18 billion, or 13 percent of farm cash receipts. They jumped by 65 percent during the 1980s to $30 billion in 1990, making these mostly labor-intensive commodities worth about one-sixth of total farm sales. It should be noted that there are several farm sales series; the 1987 census of agriculture reported that FVH sales were $17.6 billion, or 13 percent of farm cash receipts.

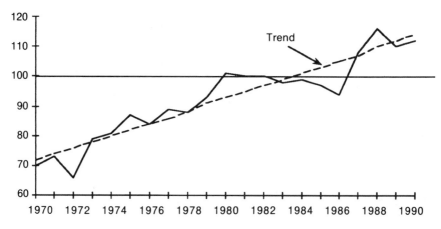

Figure 3a US fruit output, 1970–90 (1982 = 100)

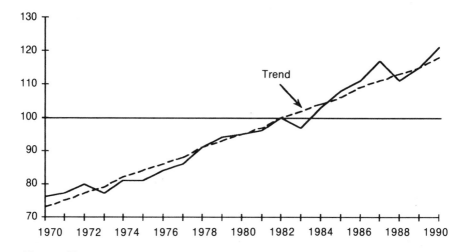

Figure 3b US vegetable and melon output, 1970–90 (1982 = 100)

Source: U.S. Department of Agriculture, Economic Research Service, unpublished data.

Fruit and vegetable production increased dramatically during the 1970s and 1980s (figure 3a and b). There are several reasons. First, consumer preferences have shifted toward fruits and vegetables. Second, the United States is a net exporter of fruits and vegetables, so that growing market demand in the United States and abroad have been largely satisfied through US production. Third, fruit and vegetable production has expanded fastest in US regions that have traditionally relied on Mexican workers, and the labor market features that lead to dependence on Mexican workers there are spreading to other areas.

The demand for immigrant farm workers depends on the domestic and export demand for FVH commodities and on whether they are picked by hand or machine. The US consumption of most farm commodities increases about 1 percent annually, about the same as the rate of population growth, but the demand for FVH commodities has been increasing by another 2 or 3 percent annually, or about as much as personal incomes typically go up, because Americans tend to spend about the same percentage on FVH commodities as their incomes rise.

Even though Americans have been increasing consumption of most fruits and vegetables, they have among the lowest levels of fruit and vegetable consumption among OECD countries (table 4). In most OECD countries, residents consume 10 to 20 percent more pounds of fruits and vegetables per person. US exports of horticultural products—primarily fruits, vegetables, and nuts—were $6.8 billion in 1992, and they are projected to reach $7.2 billion in 1993. (*The Packer*, 23 January 1993, 4). US exports of fresh fruits and vegetables are expected to increase by 7 to 10 percent annually during the 1990s, in part because of fewer trade barriers and income growth in Mexico, the fourth largest export market for US produce. California farmers, for example, exported 100 times more fresh tomatoes to Mexico in 1991 than they did in 1987, and many produce dealers expect Mexicans, who already consume more fruits and vegetables per capita than Americans, to be willing to pay a premium for higher quality produce.

Both US and foreign consumers are increasing fastest their consumption of the fresh vegetables that tend to be harvested by Mexican workers. The average American's consumption of fresh vegetables, for example, rose 23 percent, to 136 pounds per person during the 1980s, but the increase was sharpest for labor-intensive broccoli; the per capita consumption of fresh broccoli almost tripled from 1.6 to 4.5 pounds during the decade. The consumption of fresh fruit similarly also rose during the 1980s, led by increases in per capita consumption of apples, grapes, and strawberries.

Farm labor data are inadequate to provide a reliable overall link between rising US consumption and production and an increased demand-pull for Mexican workers. The tripling of fresh broccoli consumption, however, illustrates how an increase in consumption can increase the demand for Mexican workers. Broccoli is hand-harvested, and its production in California requires an average 52 hours of hired labor per acre. There was a 50 percent, or 40,000-acre, increase in US broccoli acreage during the 1980s, so 2.1 million additional hours of hired labor were needed in the United States to produce broccoli. Even though broccoli is harvested over a long season, enabling workers to

Table 4 Per capita produce consumption in OECD countries,[a] 1980 and 1988 (pounds, except where noted)

Country	Vegetables[b]			Fruit		
	1980	1988	Percentage change	1980	1988	Percentage change
Canada	328.7	344.8	5	198.2	214.7	8
France	407.9	437.0	7	158.3	177.2	12
Germany	334.0	334.0	0	250.2	256.8	3
Greece	617.1	642.6	4	272.7	242.7	−11
Italy	470.7	469.6	0	268.1	239.6	−11
Japan	314.4	329.8	5	85.8	86.2	0
Spain	571.7	536.8	−6	239.6	222.0	−7
Sweden	255.7	275.9	8	157.0	177.5	13
United Kingdom	405.0	392.9	−3	107.4	124.6	16
United States[c]	302.0	326.3	8	131.0	140.4	7
OECD average	363.1	380.5	5	185.5	183.5	−1

OECD = Organization for Economic Cooperation and Development

a. Includes fresh and processed.

b. Includes potatoes, sweet potatoes, pulses (beans), fresh vegetables and processing vegetables.

c. Because it was more complete, the source of US vegetable data is Economic Research Service, USDA.

Source: Organization for Economic Cooperation and Development, OECD Food Consumption Statistics, 1980 and 1988.

average 500 to 1,000 hours annually, the increased production of broccoli, a commodity worth just 1 percent of the total value of FVH commodities, required 2,000 to 4,000 additional seasonal workers just to handle the 1980s increase in production.

NAFTA will presumably increase US imports of FVH commodities such as broccoli, but rising consumption can permit US production and imports to rise simultaneously. The value and volume of particular imported fruits and vegetables increased dramatically during the 1980s— from 100 to 1,000 percent—but often from such low starting points that imports still have only a small share of the US market. For example, fresh broccoli imports increased tenfold during the 1980s, but they accounted for only 2 percent of US consumption in 1991. Similarly, US consumption, production, and imports of fresh tomatoes each rose by 30 to 40 percent.

US fruit and vegetable consumption should continue to increase in the 1990s. The question is whether the production of the fruits and vegetables that Americans want will shift to Mexico. As discussed in the section covering Mexican agriculture, Mexico's primary competitive advantage is climate; Mexico can produce fresh vegetables during the winter months when most US production areas except Florida are not producing. But even if Mexico completely displaces production in Florida, most fruit and vegetable production will remain in the United States because two-thirds of the production occurs in the summer and fall, when neither Mexico nor Florida is producing significant quantities. As figure 4 makes clear, even if Mexico supplied all of the fresh tomatoes consumed in the United States during its January-through-May marketing period, most fresh tomatoes would still be produced in the United States.

If fruit and vegetable production continues to expand in the United States, will crops be harvested by Americans driving machines or by Mexican workers picking crops by hand? During the late 1960s and early 1970s, after the Bracero program ended and before large-scale illegal immigration began, the ratio of farm wages to the price of farm machinery rose sharply. Growers supported so many mechanization projects at land-grant universities that the universities were accused of being virtually private research labs for them (Hightower 1978).[3] But illegal immigration slowed the increase in relative farm wages after 1975 (figure 5), and grower interest in mechanization declined. Today, most of the major fruits and vegetables grown in the United States are hand-harvested (table 5), and absent a sharp increase in farm wages, there is little prospect of mechanization.

---

3. For a critique of Hightower's argument, see Martin and Olmsted (1985, 601–06).

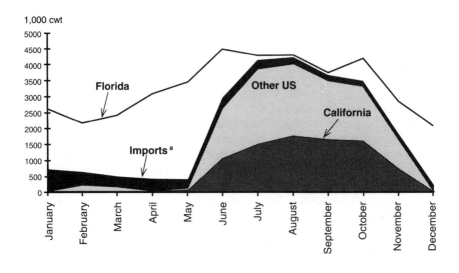

Figure 4 US shipments of tomatoes by origin, 1992

a. 95 percent of 1992 imports came from Mexico.

Source: Agricultural Marketing Service, USDA.

Agricultural engineers note that machines are available to harvest practically every fruit and vegetable grown in the United States, but that machines replace hand-pickers only when it is economically rational to make the switch—that is, when the cost of machine harvesting is cheaper than the cost of hand harvesting. The cost of machine harvesting falls as technological improvements make machines more efficient, science makes crops more amenable to machine harvesting, and packing and processing facilities become capable of handling machine-harvested produce. Since the technology of hand harvesting tends to be static, farm wages are the best indicator of the cost of hand harvesting.

Farm wages continued to fall relative to the price of machinery throughout the 1980s, reaching a postwar low in 1983–84. Since the Immigration Reform and Control Act (IRCA) was enacted in 1986, the wage-machinery index has risen slightly, but not enough to prompt widespread interest in mechanization. Indeed, as farm wages began falling in the early 1990s, grower interest in mechanizing the single most labor-intensive activity in US agriculture waned—the harvesting of raisin grapes around Fresno, California, for four to six weeks each August through September. The 50,000 seasonal workers assembled every year to earn an average $2,000 to $4,000 have been earning the same piece-rate wage throughout the 1980s—about 16 cents for cutting 25 pounds of grapes and laying them on paper to dry. Growers argue that "without

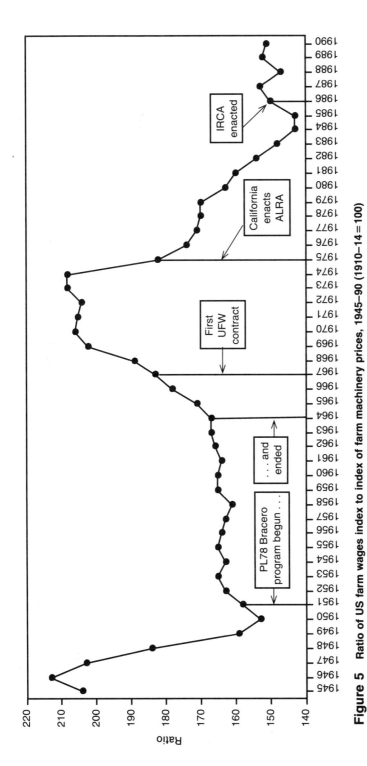

Figure 5 Ratio of US farm wages index to index of farm machinery prices, 1945–90 (1910–14 = 100)

ALRA = Agricultural Labor Relations Act.
IRCA = Immigration Reform and Control Act.
UFW = United Farm Workers
Source: US Department of Agriculture, Economic Research Service, unpublished data.

Table 5 United States: Major fruits and vegetables hand-harvested, 1990

Percentage of acreage hand-harvested	Fruits[a]	Cash receipts 1990 (millions of dollars)	Vegetables and melons[b]	Cash receipts 1990 (millions of dollars)
76–100	Apple	1,445	Cantaloupe	182
	Grape[c]	1,662	Lettuce	847
	Peach[c]	365	Asparagus	148
	Pear[c]	262	Cauliflower	190
	Strawberry	594		
	Apricot	41	Peppers	219
	Sweet cherry[c]	119	Broccoli[c]	268
	Grapefruit[c]	384	Celery	214
	Lemon[c]	278	Cabbage	121
	Plums and prunes[c]	267	Cucumber[c]	215
	Orange[c]	1,455	Mushrooms	502
			Watermelon	126
			Honeydews	82
51–75			Sweet potatoes	108
26–50			Onions	551
			Tomatoes[c]	1,622
0–25	Tart cherry[c]	37	Carrots	273
	Cranberry	153	Sweet corn[c]	467
			Dry beans	675
			Potatoes	2,678
			Peas[c]	132
			Lima beans[c]	n.a.
			Snap beans[c]	204
Total		7,062		9,416

n.a. = not available.

a. These major fruits accounted for 92 percent of the $7.7 billion value of all fruit sales in 1990.
b. US cash receipts for vegetables and melons were $11.5 billion in 1990; these major vegetables accounted for 80 percent of these receipts.
c. More than 50 percent of crop is processed.

Source: US Department of Agriculture 1992. Agriculture in a North American Free Trade Agreement. (Washington: USDA, 1992).

a foreign labor force [that maintains stable wages], the [raisin] industry could not remain competitive in the international marketplace"(Alvarado et al. 1992, 123). A mechanical harvester is available to harvest raisin grapes, but as one grower said, why spend over $100,000 on a machine to be used just a few weeks each year when two or three workers are available for each harvesting job?

Mexicanization

There are 2 million to 3 million farm workers hired in the United States during a typical year. More and more, these workers are Mexican-born, and they are increasingly likely to have arrived only a short time before. Neither American nor Mexican workers remain seasonal farm workers for a lifetime. Both groups pass through a seasonal labor market that operates like a revolving door, and this reinforces the further Mexicanization or Latinization of the farm work force through demand-pull forces on Mexico-to-US migration.

The data to document both the Latinization of the farm work force and the revolving-door farm labor market are inadequate. Farm worker advocates have long bemoaned these data inadequacies: some have alleged that the dearth of accurate data is symptomatic of the federal government's indifference to farm workers; they claim, for example, that the government has better data on migratory birds than on migratory farm workers.

There are two major federal sources of data on US farm workers, and they paint very different pictures of who does the nation's farm work. The monthly Current Population Survey (CPS) of 60,000 households includes about 1,500 who worked in agriculture during the previous week, but this household-based survey reports that most US farm workers are young white men. The National Agricultural Workers Survey (NAWS), by contrast, reports that most farm workers are recently arrived Mexican immigrants.

The CPS has traditionally collected data on farm workers by asking questions about them in December, when those migrants had presumably returned home. About 1,500 households in the December CPS included at least one farm worker throughout the 1980s. For these 1,500, data were collected on where the farm worker worked during the year as well as his farm and nonfarm earnings. The USDA analyzed the survey data to reach its 2.5 million estimate of hired US farm workers in 1985 and 1987.

These workers were 78 percent white, 14 percent Hispanic, and 8 percent black or other (box 7). White workers were the majority or plurality in every region of the United States, including the Pacific states of California, Oregon, and Washington, where white farm workers outnumbered Hispanics 54 to 44 percent.

Researchers allege frequently that the CPS household survey generates the "wrong" ethnic mix of farm workers. As evidence, they note the CPS's report that most farm workers are employed in non-labor-intensive field crop and livestock agriculture rather than in FVH agriculture. If the workers were employed in more than one commodity in the CPS, they were assigned to the commodity in which they did the most days of farm work. In 1987 only 20 percent of all hired workers—518,000 of 2.5 million—worked only or mostly in FVH commodities. Over 1.1 million workers, by contrast, worked mostly or only on grain and other field crop farms.

The CPS portrays a young, white, and male work force. In the CPS data, whites are the youngest farm workers (median age 24), largely because so many of them are 14- to 17-year-old teenagers in the Midwestern states. In the Midwest, where farmers outnumber hired workers, both groups tend to be white. However, in the regions such as the Pacific and the Southeast that produce FVH commodities, farm workers outnumber operators, and the operators tend to be white, while the hired workers tend to be minorities.

The CPS data analysis was discontinued after 1987, but a simple comparison of CPS data with Immigration and Naturalization Service (INS) data on the illegal aliens who applied for legal immigrant status under the special agricultural worker (SAW) legalization program shows sharp differences in worker characteristics. There were 1.3 million illegal aliens[4] who applied for temporary legal status under the SAW legalization program included for farm workers under IRCA; the CPS reported 326,000 Hispanic farm workers in 1985 and 338,000 in 1987. Even if all of the Hispanic farm workers in the CPS were illegal aliens, and if all of the SAW applicants qualified, the CPS apparently missed almost three Hispanic farm workers for every one that it found.

IRCA created two legalization programs: a general program (I-687), which granted legal status to illegal aliens if they had continuously resided in the United States since 1982, and the SAW farm worker program (I-700), which granted legal status to illegal aliens who did at least 90 days of farm work in 1985–86. Farmers and farm worker advocates testified that because many illegal aliens were paid in cash, it should be much easier for them to satisfy the 90-day work requirement than for nonfarm aliens to satisfy the residence requirement. A SAW applicant, for example, could have entered the United States illegally in early 1986, left after doing 90 days of farm work, and then applied for SAW status from abroad. An applicant could apply with only an employer's affidavit that the worker had done 90 days of work in virtually any crop. The burden of proof then shifted to the INS to disprove the alien's claimed employment.

The major surprise of the SAW program was the large number of applicants. Most observers estimated that 1 million to 1.5 million people did 90 or more days work on US crop farms, and of these, 10 to 40 percent were unauthorized.[5] It was on the basis of such guesses that the SAW program was divided into two parts: Group I SAWs had to do at least 90 days of qualifying work in each of years 1984, 1985, and 1986, but a maximum 350,000 such workers could be in this group, and they could convert from temporary to permanent resident-alien status after

---

4. Over 90 percent of all SAW applicants were from Western Hemisphere countries, including 82 percent from Mexico and 4 percent from Central American countries such as El Salvador.

5. For a discussion of these estimates, see Martin 1990.

one year. This 350,000 figure was a consensus estimate of the number of unauthorized aliens eligible for the SAW program.

An examination of the SAW applicant data suggests that far too many aliens claimed to have done farm work and that the CPS missed most of the Hispanic farm workers in the United States. The INS is expected to eventually approve about 1.1 million SAW applications. With the 70,000 applicants under the general legalization program who had agricultural occupations, the US government is thus acknowledging that 1.2 million mostly Hispanic workers were employed as illegal aliens in US agriculture in the mid-1980s.

IRCA also included special provisions whereby alien farm workers could be admitted if labor shortages were anticipated. The statutory formula to determine when to apply the provision led to a new survey of farm workers, the National Agricultural Workers Survey (NAWS). In the course of finding that there were no farm labor shortages, this Department of Labor–sponsored survey obtained demographic data on the workers employed in most of crop agriculture. Unlike the CPS data, which are drawn from a sample of US housing units, NAWS data are obtained from a sample of workers actually employed on farms. While the reliability of the data has not yet been established, the demographic and economic characteristics of the workers in the NAWS seem to comport well with the SAW data and with the numerous state and local surveys conducted to assess the effects of IRCA on agriculture.

The NAWS found that three-fourths of all farm workers in seasonal agricultural services (SAS) or crop agriculture[6] are minorities, usually immigrants from Mexico who have been in the United States for less than 10 years (box 8). The NAWS reported that most of these farm workers are married men who are poorly educated and who live with their families at their US work sites.

In surveys conducted between 1989 and 1991, the NAWS found that 40 percent of SAS farm workers were US citizens and 60 percent were

---

6. The NAWS covers SAS agriculture, which by regulation and court decision has been expanded to include most of US crop agriculture. IRCA states that SAS is to be defined by commodity (perishable) and activity (field work), so that those legalized under the SAW program had to have been illegal aliens who performed or supervised field work in 1985–86 related to planting, cultural practices, cultivating, growing, and harvesting fruits and vegetables of every kind and "other perishable commodities."

The definition of "perishable commodity" was stretched first by USDA and then by courts to include virtually all plants grown for human food (except sugar cane) and many nonedible plants, such as cotton, Christmas trees, cut flowers, sod grass, and Spanish reeds. Field workers include all of the paid hand- or machine-operators involved with these SAS commodities, the supervisors of field workers and equipment operators, mechanics who repair machinery, and pilots who spray crops. This means that even an illegal Central American refugee paid to work 90 days in a church's vegetable garden could qualify as a SAW applicant. The youngest SAW approved was a three-year-old who helped his parents to bunch onions in 1985–86.

aliens. The aliens included SAWs: 40 percent had "temporary resident" status, another 25 percent were permanent resident aliens, 16 percent received legal status through other programs such as political asylum, and 20 percent of the alien workers were undocumented. About 60 percent of the estimated 200,000 unauthorized alien workers arrived within the past five years, that is, after IRCA was enacted.

There are many estimates of the percentage of US farm workers who are currently unauthorized. In hearings and case studies conducted by or for the Commission on Agricultural Workers (CAW) in 1990 and 1991, it was estimated that 0 to 35 percent of the workers in particular crops were unauthorized despite the mid-1980s legalization of 1.2 million farm workers. Such estimates must be interpreted cautiously, since many are made by people who have an incentive to overestimate. For example, employers who are asked, "if IRCA were strictly enforced, would you face a shortage of labor?" have an incentive to overestimate their employment of unauthorized workers, especially if they are also advocating a program that would give them easy access to legal foreign farm workers in the event that unauthorized workers were no longer available. Nonetheless, these data indicate that illegal immigration is continuing.

As box 8 indicates, most US farm workers are poor immigrants from Mexico. According to the NAWS, farm workers averaged $180 weekly for 26 weeks for annual farm earnings of $4,665, about 72 percent of the $6,465 poverty-level income of an individual in 1990. Farm workers average another 10 weeks of unemployment searching for farm and nonfarm jobs.

Over one-third of the farm workers in the NAWS also did nonfarm work. Even though it paid slightly less per hour than farm work, most workers interviewed while doing farm work said they preferred nonfarm work—most wanted to eventually find nonfarm jobs despite the fact that their hourly earnings were higher in agriculture. Nonfarm work in services such as janitorial or clean-up businesses or in construction was felt by many farm workers to be more stable and to offer them more opportunities for upward mobility.

The NAWS also suggests how the farm worker force is changing. Two trends seem important for assessing the impact of NAFTA on the demand-pull of jobs in rural America. First, immigrants are a larger share of recent farm work force entrants than they are of the entire farm work force, suggesting that new entrants tend to come from abroad. Second, Mexican immigrants appear to be spreading throughout US agriculture. Mexican immigrants and Mexican-Americans have long dominated the seasonal farm work forces of California, Texas, and other Southwestern states, and they have spread to Florida since the 1970s. However, the NAWS and other surveys suggest that an unintended consequence of IRCA has been to spread immigrant Mexican workers throughout US agriculture so that Mexican immigrants are rapidly replacing whites and blacks in the tobacco fields of North Carolina, Puerto Ricans in New York and New Jersey, and white teenagers in Iowa. Mexican workers are also appearing in nonfarm jobs from meat packing to construction throughout the Midwest. This current "Mexicanization" of rural and middle America is evidence that the demand-pull of US jobs persists for Mexicans in the 1990s.

The Revolving Door

Farm workers do not remain farm workers, whether they are US citizens or legal or illegal aliens; this explains the folk-saying that it is hard to find a farm worker over 40.[7] Of 2 million to 3 million hired farm workers,

---

7. Farming requires a significant investment, which explains the other half of this aphorism; it is hard to find a farmer under 40.

- Median earnings were $4.85 per hour; work weeks averaged 37 hours for SAS earnings of $180 and, for 26 weeks, $4,665.
- Less than half of the workers have unemployment insurance and workers' compensation coverage; 21 percent have off-the-job health insurance.
- 28 percent live in employer-provided housing.

Other work and income. Farm workers are poor but not dependent on welfare.

- 46 percent of all SAS workers have below poverty-level incomes; the poverty rate is highest for unauthorized workers (77 percent).
- 36 percent also do non-SAS farm work; such work paid a median $4.50 per hour and is preferred to farm work.
- 58 percent are unemployed during the year; 50 percent of these unemployed are jobless less than two months; only 28 percent of the jobless farm workers apply for unemployment insurance.
- 40 percent of the workers spend an average 19 weeks abroad each year.
- Median individual incomes are $5,000 to $7,500; median family incomes are $7,500 to $10,000; 50 percent of the families are below the 1989 poverty line of $12,675 for a family of four.
- 55 percent of the workers own assets, usually a vehicle.
- 16 percent get food stamps, 3 percent Aid to Families with Dependent Children.

This profile is based on quarterly interviews with 7,242 farm workers (for some questions) employed in seasonal agricultural services between the fall of 1989 and 1991. SAS encompasses mostly crop agriculture: it probably includes 80 percent of all farm workers, 70 percent of all farm jobs, and 60 percent of farm wages paid.

Source: Mines et al. 1991. (These data are preliminary, and their interpretation is my own.)

---

1 million to 2 million satisfy at least one of the many definitions of migrant and seasonal farm workers (MSFWs)—migrants are people who must establish a second home to do farm work, and seasonals are those who are employed less than six months on farms (Martin and Martin 1993, chapters 2 and 5). With a 5 to 10 percent annual exit from the farm work force, 50,000 to 200,000 newcomers must join the work force each year to keep the MSFW work force at full strength.

Given agriculture's revolving-door labor market, it is not surprising that farmers exert continuing pressure to obtain immigrant farm workers via temporary worker programs or through illegal alien channels. NAFTA does not address unauthorized immigration, although President Salinas has said on several occasions that, after NAFTA is approved, Mexico will seek negotiations on migration. Other Mexican leaders, including 1988 presidential candidate Cuauhtemoc Cardenas, argued that improved protection for Mexican workers in the United States should be an integral part of NAFTA negotiations.

There have been no such negotiations during NAFTA talks nor in the side agreements negotiated during the summer of 1993. Nonetheless, the evidence points to a continued influx of unauthorized Mexican workers into the US farm work force. One indicator of the continued presence of illegal aliens in the US farm work force appeared during the implementation of IRCA. If the departure of SAW workers led to farm labor shortages, the US attorney general was empowered to admit replenishment agricultural workers (RAWs) to replace them. In order to have a list of such workers to contact in the event of labor shortages, the INS had a signup period for those interested in obtaining RAW visas. Publicity to attract potential RAW workers was carried out in the countries from which the most SAWs came. Yet most of those signing up for RAW visas in the fall of 1989 were already US residents; almost 90 percent of the 600,000 applicants for RAW visas were US residents.

There is also other evidence that IRCA did not stop the influx of illegal aliens into the US farm work force. After IRCA was enacted in 1986, farm labor contractors (FLCs) greatly expanded their roles in many farm labor markets. FLCs are the intermediaries who, for a fee, recruit, transport, and supervise farm workers, and today they match more than 50 percent of seasonal workers and jobs in many harvest labor markets. Worker, farmer, and agency testimony as well as research suggest that FLCs are practically a proxy for the employment of undocumented workers and egregious or subtle violations of labor laws (Commission on Agricultural Workers 1992).

The increase in FLC activities has been driven by several factors, including farmer efforts to minimize the risk that the INS may enforce laws against hiring illegal aliens on their farms, the arrival of immigrant workers from Guatemala and southern Mexico since 1986, and the legalization of people with the requisite experience to get into the FLC game. IRCA's employer sanctions increased the potential cost of hiring illegal alien workers, so growers tried to shift these risks to FLCs since they, under IRCA, are employers in their own right. Second, the immigrants arriving since IRCA was enacted have in many cases needed nontraditional intermediaries for language, recruitment, or social-service reasons—farmers used to dealing with Mexicans from the Central Highlands were not necessarily capable of dealing with the southern Mexican Mixtecs and Guatemalan Indians arriving today. Third, the SAW program legalized more people who could be FLCs; FLC registration usually requires legal status, and some newly legalized SAWs became FLCs.

FLCs, the control of illegal immigration, and the enforcement of labor standards seem to be mutually incompatible. A contractor operates between a farmer and a farm worker, but the power of the two over the contractor is very different. Farmers typically know what the going overhead or commission for performing a farm task is, and thus FLCs are unlikely to extract an extra-high fee from them. Newly arrived immigrants, on the other hand, may not know the minimum wage, so FLCs can turn what appears to be a money-losing deal with farmers into a profit-making deal by extracting money from workers. As the US Industrial Commission observed as long ago as 1901 (p. 320–21), "the position of the contractor . . . is peculiarly that of an organizer and employer of immigrants. . . . He holds his own mainly because of his ability to get cheap labor . . . [he] succeeds because he lives among the poorest class of people, knows them personally, knows their circumstances, and can drive the hardest kind of bargain with them."

IRCA was enacted to reduce illegal immigration by making it more difficult for unauthorized workers to find US jobs and to offer a legal immigration status to certain unauthorized aliens. In agriculture, IRCA was a case of good intentions gone awry—it made the enforcement of immigration laws more difficult in US agriculture, it signaled farmers that foreign workers would continue to be made available, and it spread knowledge about how to work "legally" in the United States throughout rural Mexico. Until IRCA, INS enforcement in agriculture usually involved the Border Patrol driving into fields and apprehending aliens who tried to run away. Farmers pointed out that the INS was required to obtain search warrants before inspecting factories for illegal aliens, and they successfully argued that the INS should similarly be obliged to show evidence that illegal aliens were employed on a farm before raiding it. IRCA subsequently extended the search warrant requirement.

IRCA converted enforcement in agriculture from the pursuit of aliens in the field to a paper chase. As a result, there are far fewer farm worker apprehensions despite what appear to be pre-IRCA levels of illegal alien employment. Many employers of seasonal farm workers leave hiring to a field supervisor or foreman so that when work begins at 6 or 7 a.m., INS employment verification forms are completed, each worker provides a copy of his or her work authorization, and then the form and the copy of the green card and driver's license are returned to the office to be available for INS inspection. The INS has been unable to inspect enough employer offices or impose enough fines to change employer and alien behavior.

Before IRCA, illegal-alien farm workers were often called undocumented workers because they did not have documents authorizing them to work in the United States. IRCA changed unauthorized farm workers into "documented illegal aliens." Today's "documented illegals" have the work authorization documents (usually an I-551 green card and a driver's license) needed to be employed legally in the United States, although these documents are generally purchased for $30 to $50, not issued by the US government.

Rural Mexicans, usually the poorest and least sophisticated illegal aliens in the United States before IRCA, have now learned that they can get jobs with purchased work authorization documents. IRCA may well be remembered as a stimulus to illegal immigration because it spread work authorization documents and knowledge about them to very poor and unsophisticated rural Mexicans and Central Americans, encouraging first-time entrants from these areas. Some evidence suggests that the aliens know their green cards are fraudulent since many continue to cross the US border without inspection and use their green cards only to get a US job.

This flow of rural Mexicans and Central Americans stimulated by IRCA implies that demand-pull factors in rural America stand ready to draw displaced rural Mexicans into US labor markets, especially if NAFTA creates a supply push from rural Mexico in the 1990s.

Even if NAFTA is not put in place, however, the demand-pull of jobs for rural Mexicans should persist during the 1990s because, first, the US consumption of fruits, vegetables, and labor-intensive items such as flowers is expected to expand. Since there has been a significant slowdown in research on labor-saving ways of producing these crops, the US need for seasonal workers to tend and harvest these crops—two-thirds of whom are currently immigrants from Mexico—is likely to continue to increase. Second, the entire US farm labor market is becoming more dependent on recently arrived immigrant workers from Mexico, an unintended side effect of IRCA. Finally, higher expectations and ever-improving communications are helping immigrant farm workers escape from the US farm labor market. If the revolving-door farm labor market turns faster in the 1990s, more rural Mexicans will find their way into the US economy through the agricultural port of entry.

5

Supply-Push in Mexico in the 1990s

During the 1980s, rural Mexicans responded to the demand-pull of jobs in US agriculture because the Mexican work force was growing extraordinarily fast while Mexican farmers faced a cost-price squeeze, making farming there less attractive. At the same time, Mexico's urban economy was offering almost no new "real" jobs to those pushed out of rural areas. The demand for labor in the United States found a ready match among disillusioned and unemployed rural Mexicans, who flocked across the border. A culture of migration took hold in many rural areas of Mexico; young men were expected to go north to earn money, making emigration a normal part of coming of age.

If passed, NAFTA eventually will reduce the supply-push forces in rural Mexico that encourage emigration. However, NAFTA is expected to accelerate economic changes already under way in rural Mexico, increasing supply-push emigration factors in the 1990s. In addition, the well-developed networks that link rural Mexico and rural America can translate supply-push pressures into more migration.

The expectation that the same trade and investment policies needed to reduce emigration pressures lead to a migration hump or spike in the short run was the major finding of the US Commission for the Study of International Migration and Cooperative Economic Development. The commission (1990, 28) nonetheless urged the United States to "expedite the development of a US-Mexico free trade area." The commission, however, did not deal with the size or duration of the expected Mexico-to-US migration hump.

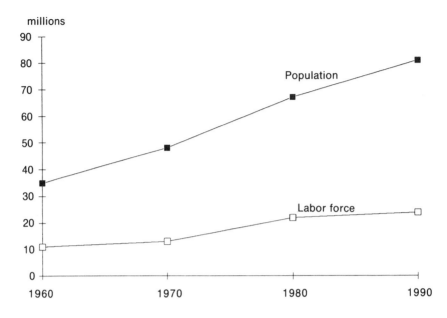

millions

Figure 6 Mexico: population and labor force, 1960–90
Source: Mexican Census Bureau.

Mexican Population and Labor Force Trends

Mexico is the world's 11th most populous country; its 1990 population of 81 million to 88 million puts the country's population between that of larger Bangladesh and of Germany. However, the range in the estimated population is indicative of the problems in projecting Mexico's current and future population and labor force. However, several things are clear: Mexico is currently the world's major emigration country, sending 200,000 to 300,000 citizens "permanently" abroad each year; its population is growing by about 1.8 million annually, and its labor force is growing by 900,000 per year; and the Mexican economy, which offers about 10 million formal-sector jobs to a work force of 30 million, has been creating only about 300,000 to 400,000 such jobs annually. The data in figure 6 report the population and labor force as measured by the Mexican census of population (COP). The population rose by almost 40 percent in the 1960s and 1970s, but the population growth rate appears to have dropped sharply in the 1980s.

The apparent sharp drop in Mexican population growth means that there will be less-rapid labor force growth after 2000, and thus less demographic pressure for job creation or emigration. However, it is not clear that the population growth rate slowed as much during the 1980s as the Mexican COP indicates. The 1980 census enumerated 69 million people and, based on this count, the estimated population of Mexico in 1990 was projected by the Mexican Census Bureau to be 86 million to 89 million. The World Bank estimated that Mexico's 1990 population would be 86 million, and the US Agency for International Development projected 88 million Mexicans.

When Mexico's 1990 COP enumerated only 81 million people, there was a debate over whether the "missing" 5 million to 7 million people are living in Mexico but simply were not counted, whether Mexican fertility and thus population growth dropped more than expected during the 1980s, or whether several million Mexicans settled in the United States during the 1980s. The consensus so far seems to be that all three factors played a role in the lower-than-expected number of Mexicans counted in 1990: the census undercount has been estimated to be 2 million to 6 million; the fertility of Mexican women seems to have dropped sharply, from almost seven births per woman in the 1970s to four today; and 1.5 million to 3 million Mexicans may have emigrated permanently in the 1980s. If all resident Mexicans had been enumerated in the 1990 COP, the Mexican population would have been, according to these estimates, 83 million to 87 million.[1]

The size and growth of the Mexican population determine the number of Mexicans seeking jobs 15 to 20 years later. Rapid population growth of almost 3 percent annually during the 1970s produced the 1 million plus labor force entrants of today. Mexico's population growth rate has fallen, but there is disagreement over how much, and thus what the flow of migrants from Mexico to the United States may be after 2000, with or without NAFTA. The Mexican census reports that the population growth rate was 2.6 percent annually in 1980, so that there were 1.8 million more Mexicans each year. By 1990, the census reported a 2.3 percent growth rate, implying an additional 2 million Mexicans annually if the population in 1990 was 86 million. The World Bank has projected a slowing of population growth in Mexico to 1.8 percent annually in the 1990s, which would give Mexico a population of 103 million in 2000.

The exact size and growth of Mexico's population may not be known, but there is no doubt that it is growing at least twice as fast as the US population, which is growing 1 percent annually. Furthermore, the Mexican population is much younger than the US population: 38 percent of Mexicans are younger than 15 versus 22 percent of Americans.

---

1. Demographers at the Population Reference Bureau report that Mexico's mid-1993 population was 90 million, and at their estimated 2.3 percent growth rate, the Mexican population is projected to be 118 million in 2010, suggesting a net addition to the population of 1 million annually. PRB estimates that 71 percent of the Mexican population was urban in 1993, suggesting that 26 million Mexicans were rural residents.

Mexico's population grew much faster in the 1960s and 1970s,[2] and the labor force felt the impact of this baby boom in the 1980s. The Mexican COP reports that Mexico's labor force grew half as fast as the population during the 1960s, twice as fast as the population during the 1970s, and half as fast as the undercounted population during the 1980s. A comparison of Mexican population and labor force trends highlights two points (figure 6). First, Mexico has an extraordinarily low labor force participation rate: in most industrial countries, half of the total population is in the labor force, but in Mexico, less than one-third are employed or seeking work. Second, the labor force participation rate fell during the 1980s as discouraged workers gave up the search for jobs that did not exist. Mexico added 10 million to 15 million people in the 1960s and 1970s, but the Mexican labor force increased by only 2 million during the 1980s. There is also disagreement over the size of the Mexican labor force: the 1990 labor force was reported to be 24 million in the COP and 30 million by the Mexican Ministry of Labor.

The Mexican employment problem has been described as a case of too many new labor force entrants, too much informal employment (that is, not in wage and salaried jobs) in the urban areas where most of the population lives, and too many poor farmers. Mexico will have about 1 million new job seekers each year during the 1990s, and to absorb them, Mexico's GDP must grow, by one estimate, by at least 6 percent annually (Cornelius 1991, 11). Mexico's GDP in 1990 was $238 billion, and a real 6 percent growth rate would add $14.3 billion annually to GDP, implying that the cost in additional GDP to create each new job in Mexico is $14,300. Such an economic growth rate would require very high levels of foreign investment.

Mexicans have been migrating from rural to urban areas for decades. During the 1980s the urban population grew at a faster rate (2.9 percent) than the total population, leaving Mexico with almost three-fourths of its population in urban areas. Mexico City is one of the world's largest cities, and its 15 million to 20 million residents are 20 to 25 percent of the country's population.[3] About the same percentage of Mexicans (32

---

2. US demographer Ansley Coale noted (1978, 422–23) that Mexico during the 1960s and 1970s "presents a puzzling picture for those who expound a simple version of the demographic transition; . . . the theory that . . . countries with rapid population growth need have no concern about it because social and economic progress automatically brings down birth rates. . . . Per capita income had nearly doubled in 20 years. . . nevertheless, fertility in 1975 was, if anything, somewhat higher than it was 20 years before." Mexico's failure to experience the expected demographic transition "is widely attributed to unequal distribution of the benefits of that development" (Nagel 1978, 11).

3. The World Bank reports that 23 percent of Mexico's 1990 population of 86.3 million live in Mexico City, implying 20 million residents. However, the 1990 Mexican COP found only 15 million people in Mexico City, a number defended by the census director as a reflection of September 1985 earthquakes and public and private decentralization efforts.

percent) lived in cities of 1 million or more in 1990 as did Americans (36 percent). However, despite urbanization, Mexico's rural population was larger in 1990 than it was in 1980.

Although the rural share of Mexico's population (28 percent) is about the same as the rural share of the US population (25 percent), most of Mexico's 22 million to 26 million rural residents live on farms, while fewer than 10 percent of the 63 million rural residents of the United States are in farming families. In Mexico, the rural population generates only 9 percent of GDP, and rural incomes are less than one-third of Mexico's $2,500 per capita GDP. US agriculture, by contrast, generates a slightly larger share of GDP than farmers' share of the population, so US farmers have higher-than-average incomes.

Low farm incomes have sharply reduced Mexico's rural population, and the persisting rural-urban income gap continues to encourage rural-urban migration. By one estimate, about one-fourth of Mexico's 30 million labor force of almost 8 million adults are farmers or farm workers, a 25 percent increase from almost 6 million in 1980. In 1980, five-sixths of the workers employed in agriculture were men, and half of them were self-employed. The projected behavior of these farmers, farm workers, and their dependents in the 1990s may be the most important factor to explain NAFTA's impact on Mexico-to-US migration.

Mexican Agriculture

Agriculture is not a Mexican success story. Between 1945 and 1965, Mexico's agricultural output rose by 6.6 percent annually, largely as a result of improved wheat varieties and the modernization of commercial farms. Between 1966 and 1979, farm output rose by only 2.2 percent per year, less than the population growth rate, and Mexico switched from being a net food exporter to a net food importer. The Mexican government isolated agriculture from both the domestic and international economies, and by maintaining an overvalued exchange rate, discouraged both imports of modern farm inputs and exports of Mexican farm commodities.

In the late 1970s and early 1980s, the Mexican government raised the prices it guarantees farmers for the commodities they grew significantly, increased input subsidies, and saw the growth in farm output double to 4.4 percent. But this policy of buying at high prices and then selling government-owned corn and beans at low prices to urban consumers was not sustainable after the economic crisis of 1982. The Mexican government after 1982 began to reduce farm subsidies, and farm output subsequently increased at only 1.3 percent annually (less than the population growth rate). Mexico became a food-importing nation (table 6).

Table 6   Mexican agriculture, 1970–88

	1970	1975	1980	1985	1988[a]
Population (millions)	52.8	61.2	69.6	78.5	85.9
Percentage in agriculture	44	41	37	34	32
Total labor force (millions)[b]	14.9	18.4	22.8	26.8	29.3
Percentage in agriculture	44	40	36	33	31
GNP (millions of dollars)	37.5	83.3	161.5	171.0	148.7
Annual rate of growth (percentage)	3.2	3.0	2.6	2.4	2.3
GNP per capita (dollars)	710	1,360	2,320	2,180	1,770
Peso-dollar exchange rate	12.5	12.5	23.0	256.9	2,461
Total debt (millions of dollars)	n.a.	16.6	57.4	96.9	106
Crop land (millions of acres)	56.8	58.8	60.5	61.0	61.0
Irrigated land (millions of acres)	8.9	11.1	12.3	13.0	12.5
Agriculture exports (millions of dollars)	695	973	1,833	1,783	2,425
Fruits and vegetables (millions of dollars)	140	180	370	321	318
Agriculture Imports (millions of dollars)	222	936	3,168	2,325	2,877
Corn (millions of dollars)	58	405	589	255	450

n.a. = not available.

a. A few items are 1989 data.
b. Defined as the economically active population employed full-time.

Source: US Department of Agriculture, World Agriculture, Trends and Indicators, 1970–89, Statistical Bulletin Number 815, 1990, p. 355–58.

Mexico's roller coaster agricultural policies have left it with a segmented farm structure and a great deal of rural poverty. Two-thirds of Mexico's poor people are farmers and farm workers, and three-fourths of Mexico's extremely poor people live in rural areas (Levy and van Wijnbergen 1992, 498). Mexicans have been fleeing this rural poverty for decades, explaining why the urban population in Mexico is growing and why Mexicans migrate to the United States. Mexico's market-oriented economic policies are accelerating the push out of rural Mexico, and NAFTA, by reinforcing them, should also add to rural emigration pressures. However, NAFTA adds only a small increment to a historically high level of rural exodus.

This section provides a brief overview of Mexico's agricultural system, explores the extent to which NAFTA can promote job creation in rural Mexico by encouraging the production there of fruits and vegetables for export to the United States, and then discusses ways to improve economic efficiency as well as reduce rural poverty.

A Portrait of Rural Mexico

Most observers put Mexican farmers into one of four major groups. Most important for job creation and production for export are the large commercial farmers. There are perhaps 400,000 such farms—10 percent of Mexico's farms—that hire at least one laborer for one month or more. These farmers act as profit-making businesses, in contrast to the many small communal and subsistence farms; they weigh prices and costs to determine what to plant and stand ready to invest outside of agriculture if there are no profits to be made. Commercial farms cultivate about half of Mexico's farmland and are dominant in Mexico's northwestern states. They grow most of Mexico's fruits and vegetables destined for export, as well as wheat and corn, rice, sugar, tobacco, and coffee.

Commercial farmers were until 1992 limited by Article 27 of Mexico's constitution to a maximum 100 hectares (247 acres) of irrigated land to grow grains and corn, 300 hectares (720 acres) of irrigated land for orchards, or enough land to maintain 500 head of cattle.

However, farmers routinely evaded these restrictions on land ownership by having each family member own the maximum number of acres, and then the family farmed the land as a single unit. Such extended land holdings were not secure; the Mexican Constitution permitted the expropriation of "excess land" and its redistribution to the landless families who sometimes occupied it. This threat of expropriation is cited frequently to explain why there has been so little private investment in agriculture: investment is just 2 percent of farm output, versus 15 percent of output for the entire economy. A January 1992 amendment to Article 27 of the Mexican Constitution ended the right of the landless to claim excess private lands for themselves and permitted both foreigners and corporations to buy land in Mexico.

The second type of Mexican farm is the small family farm that uses family members to produce for the family's subsistence and the market. There are about 1 million such farms, and they control about 40 percent of Mexico's farmland. Many of these small farmers cultivate *ejido* or communal land (see section below), on which they grow corn and beans for their families. They sell any excess to the Mexican government, if government purchasing facilities (CONASUPO) are nearby.

The largest of these small farms operate like commercial farms if they have access to credit, technology, and markets; they switch between corn and other crops on the basis of which promises the highest return. The smallest family farms aim to produce what the family consumes and to sell only the surplus, so that their planting decisions are influenced by both family needs and market considerations. Members of small family farm households often supplement their farm earnings by working for wages in local or distant labor markets.

The largest group in rural Mexico are subsistence farmers. These 1.5 million farmers, concentrated in the north central and southern states, produce the corn and beans on which their families depend. Most purchase no inputs, have little flexibility to produce crops other than corn and beans, and many do not produce a surplus to sell to the government agency, CONASUPO, which buys crops from Mexican farmers at higher than world market prices, so they do not benefit from government price guarantees for corn and beans. If they do not produce a surplus to sell to the government and then are too far from a government outlet to buy subsidized tortillas, they are hurt by Mexico's high corn price guarantees.

Subsistence farmers are about half of Mexico's farmers, but they control only about 10 percent of the farmland. Their main source of cash income has been and remains off-farm work: many are migrant workers who shuttle into and out of the United States from home bases in low cost-of-living rural areas of Mexico. Much of the migration research done in rural Mexico over the past two decades has explained how these subsistence households rationally allocate their labor between local and distant labor markets. Many such households, for example, send young women to jobs in urban Mexico and young men to US jobs (Taylor 1987; Grindle 1988).

The fourth group in rural Mexico are landless workers. There are probably 600,000 to 700,000 such workers, although estimates range as high as 3 million. These households have no land on which to produce crops: they survive by working in local and distant labor markets. These households are most likely to be in extreme poverty, defined in one study as an income of less than $232 annually (CEPAL 1989). Landless workers are distributed in a fashion similar to *ejidatarios*, that is, they are everywhere except the Pacific Northwest.

Ejidos and Migration

The distinguishing feature of the Mexican agricultural system is that it includes private farmers, *ejidatario* members of *ejido* communal farms, and landless rural workers. The private farmers have been the beneficiaries of many government investments in agriculture, including dams and other irrigation facilities in the vegetable-exporting states of Sinaloa and Sonora. But the Mexican Revolution was fought to provide land for the peasants, and the *ejido* system was Mexico's unique land tenure system that came out of that struggle.

Ejidos are communal farms. Under Article 27 of the Mexican Constitution of 1917, Mexico's agrarian reform ministry was given the power to redistribute large private land holdings to *ejidos* and then grant *ejidatario* members and their heirs rights to the land as long as they actively worked and lived on it. *Ejidatarios* receive land as a group, but in most cases land is farmed individually. *Ejidatarios* could not sell, rent, or borrow money using the land as collateral. *Ejidos* control about 70 percent of Mexico's cropland and half of its irrigated land. Two recent policy changes may break this link to the land. First, *ejidatarios* now have the right to sell or rent their land. Second, a large number of rural Mexicans have recently received legal US immigrant status. As a result, a sojourner population anchored to rural Mexico may begin to sever its ties in the 1990s, increasing migration to the United States.

President Salinas on 7 November 1991 proposed a constitutional amendment that permits *ejido* land to be sold, rented, or used as collateral for loans. For the first time in decades, foreign and domestic corporations can own Mexican farmland. These changes to the Mexican constitution were approved on 6 January 1992.

There is considerable speculation about how *ejido* reforms will affect farmers and workers, farm output, and foreign and domestic investment, and job creation in Mexican agriculture. The major purpose of the reforms was to increase economic efficiency. Farmers everywhere respond to price incentives and, in a bid to reduce rural poverty, Mexico on several occasions raised the guaranteed price of corn. As a result, commercial and family farmers have switched to corn: for example, in Sinaloa and Sonora, corn production increased from 200,000 tons in the late 1990s to 2 million tons in 1993, largely because the guaranteed price of corn reached 2.15 times the US price. Exports of vegetables fell as a result in 1993, and in response Mexico drastically reduced corn imports (speech by Luis Tellez, undersecretary for planning, Mexican Ministry of Agriculture and Hydraulic Reources, before seminar at University of California–San Diego, 13–14 May 1993).

The gap between high producer prices and subsidized consumer prices distorts farm production, is expensive to the government, and does little to remedy rural poverty (Levy and van Wijnbergen 1992). As a result,

Mexican policymakers have recently advanced plans to change their agricultural policies to make them more efficient and equitable. The plan is simple: substitute income transfers for price guarantees. Without artificially high corn prices, commercial and family farmers would plant crops in which Mexico has a comparative advantage, such as vegetables. With an income transfer system, Mexico can more effectively assist the subsistence farmers, who the current price support system has often hurt rather than helped (Taylor 1993).

If implemented as planned, the Mexican government would make direct payments to producers of corn and 11 other field crops based on farmer-reported production histories. This payment would reflect past average yields and the difference between the current support price of corn ($750 new pesos in mid-1993 per ton) and the world price ($450 new pesos). Checks for producers would substitute for the government agencies that now influence economic activities in rural Mexico.

There are formidable challenges to be worked out before Mexico can implement this complement to *ejido* reform, ranging from whether a farmer would have to continue producing the crop to get a check (with yields expected to fall due to lower prices), whether the farmer should be required to grow another crop, or whether the land should remain idle. There is also the mundane task of issuing 3 million to 4 million checks to rural peasants in areas without reliable mail and banking services. Finally, direct payments to producers do not help landless workers, who might migrate as jobs disappear in rural areas.

Mexico is on the verge of completing major policy changes that will affect the rural areas from which most US-bound migrants originate. The effects of these land and farm policy changes on migration are hard to predict: however, no one argues that they will make it less likely that Mexicans emigrate. While it may take time for *ejido* land to be surveyed so that it can be sold, and even though Mexico's new farm policies can be designed to temporarily discourage emigration, an active land market and lower prices for the major crops will ultimately reduce the Mexican farm population. Before exploring likely opportunities for displaced farmers in urban Mexico, a survey of NAFTA's potential to create jobs in rural Mexico is in order.

NAFTA and Rural Job Creation in Mexico

Ejido and farm policy reforms in conjunction with NAFTA are expected to step up investments in rural Mexico that create jobs there for potential migrants. NAFTA and Mexican reforms should lead to some job creation in rural Mexico, but not as soon as many people hope and not enough jobs to stop emigration. For example, changing land ownership laws may not "generate a major increase in foreign investment, as investors have already found ways to work around" previous restrictions (Cook et al. 1991, 23). Investors who want to buy or rent newly available *ejido* land must in any event wait. Not all of the *ejido* land has been surveyed to determine exactly who owns what, and administrative details, such as whether one *ejidatario* can dispose of his land if the other *ejido* members object, are still being worked out.

Mexicans farm policy reforms and NAFTA should eventually increase the production of labor-intensive fruits and vegetables, a sector in which Mexico should have a comparative advantage. But Mexico's major comparative advantage in fruit and vegetable farming is climate: Mexico can produce fruits and vegetables during the winter months, when US production areas (except Florida) are idle (Cook et al. 1991). About three-fourths of US fruits and vegetables are produced in the spring, summer, and fall, when Mexico is not producing; this is why most of North America's labor-intensive fruits and vegetables will continue to be produced in the United States.

Much of the winter US vegetable production is likely to shift to Mexico, but perhaps not as fast as some observers hope. The most comprehensive study of Mexican versus US production costs (Cook et al. 1991, 458–59 and 464) concluded that there are many factors that argue against US producers shifting to Mexico:

> Mexico does not currently pose a major competitive threat [to US producers] in many horticultural crops, such as: table grapes, fresh broccoli and cauliflower, processing tomatoes, peaches, apples, strawberries, melons, and eggplant. This is generally due to a technology gap and rising Mexican costs. Much of Mexico's production is complementary to US production and serves to provide a stable year-round supply of fresh fruits and vegetables to the US consumer. Mexico's ability to expand exports is limited by the rapid growth in its own population— which is improving its diet and will be consuming more fresh fruits and vegetables as incomes rise. . . .
>
> Mexico's principal disadvantage is the technology gap . . . which is frequently reflected in lower yields in Mexico. . . . While per acre growing costs are often lower in Mexico, per unit production costs are often similar to US levels [because of lower Mexican yields]. . . .
>
> Mexico has higher marketing costs caused by the imperatives of exporting, including transportation costs to reach the US market. Also, while labor rates are lower in Mexico, labor is frequently less productive, due to restrictive work rules and other factors. Consequently, total labor costs per crop in Mexico are frequently not as low as the wage rates would suggest. In some Mexican production regions labor is becoming less available, while this is generally not true in California.
>
> Most importantly, Mexican horticultural exporters face costs that are increasing at a more rapid pace than production and marketing costs faced by US growers. The Mexican government is embarked on a program to reduce or eliminate production subsidies. . . . Mexican horticultural exporters now import a substantial portion of their inputs, such as fertilizer, boxes, seeds, transplants, equipment, plastic and chemicals. They must pay Mexican import duties on these items of from 10 to 20 percent. Further, the peso has been overvalued since

mid-1987, decreasing the competitiveness of exporters by making their products more expensive in dollar terms. . . .

The important item in location-of-production decisions is the cost per unit, not wages, and Mexican costs of production are sometimes higher than US costs despite lower wages. For example, in 1991–92, the cost of producing a 25-pound carton of fresh tomatoes was $6.53 in Mexico and $6.40 in Florida. Not only were production costs lower in Florida; Florida tomatoes typically command a $2 per box premium, further reinforcing the Florida advantage. Mexican farm wages are $4 to $6 per day, compared with $4 to $6 per hour in the United States, but Mexican farmers pay proportionately more for worker transportation, housing, and related benefits. Mexican workers in Mexico are less productive than US workers. Lower productivity, higher nonwage costs, and lower yields combine to make costs of production for many fruits and vegetables that are shipped long distances as high or higher in Mexico than in the United States.

Over the longer term, Mexican yields and worker productivity will undoubtedly rise, inducing Mexican and foreign investors to create jobs in an expanding Mexican fruit and vegetable industry. But how fast will such investments flow to rural Mexico? Not as fast as US critics fear and Mexicans hope. US agribusiness in 1991 had a relatively small investment in Mexican agriculture; only $30 million to $100 million, or less than California apricot farmers have invested in land to produce apricots. There are several good reasons why US agribusiness has avoided more direct investments in Mexico. In many instances, US growers advanced money to Mexican partners that was never repaid. However, a more important factor is the high cost of Mexican production (*The Packer*, 25 April 1992, 1A). Indeed, after five years in Mexico, the second largest US vegetable grower ceased operations there with the observation that "we can even produce more efficiently for the Mexican market from the US" (*Ag Alert*, 14 July 1993, 28). These stories in the farm press are probably more accurate reflections of the near-term prospects for US agribusiness investment in Mexico than press accounts that "California growers are frightened" by competition from Mexican fruits and vegetables as a result of NAFTA (*New York Times*, 15 August 1992, A1 and A20).

There has been a tendency to hope that NAFTA will lead to a rush of foreign investment because of what happened in a few very special cases, especially frozen broccoli and cauliflower. These commodities, which account for more than 90 percent of the frozen vegetables imported from Mexico, generate seasonal employment for 20,000 to 25,000 Mexicans in El Bajio, a region about 200 miles north of Mexico City. American processors such as Birdseye and Green Giant developed or expanded freezer plants in the region during the 1980s, and as a result, the US-produced share of the frozen broccoli and cauliflower consumed here fell from the 70 to 90 percent range in 1980 to between 40 and 50 percent in 1990. However, as noted in chapter 4, the rapid growth in per capita broccoli and cauliflower consumption has led to almost a tripling of the US production for the fresh market during the 1980s. US growers want to produce these commodities for the more profitable fresh market and send only surplus production to the processing market. In this sense, they have been willing to cede the frozen market to Mexico.

Frozen vegetables may not be typical of the changes NAFTA and foreign investment may bring to rural Mexico. Mexicans consume few frozen vegetables, both because they lack freezers and because they traditionally make frequent shopping trips for fresh vegetables. Mexico might emerge as a major supplier of frozen vegetables to the North American market, but most of the jobs and profits in these commodities are likely to remain in the fresh segment of the industry that has been expanding in the United States.

The Mexican peso is currently considered overvalued, so that a devaluation would encourage production for the US in Mexico. But over the longer term, NAFTA is expected to benefit Mexican consumers as a rising peso, supported by foreign investment in Mexico, lowers prices on imported goods. Hufbauer and Schott (1992, 57), for example, projected a 29 percent increase in the real peso exchange rate due to NAFTA, and such a peso appreciation would raise Mexican production costs far more than costs would fall through the elimination of tariffs, which averaged 8 percent on Mexican fruits and vegetables exported to the United States in 1990.

There are few predictions of how fast Mexican produce exports might rise as a result of NAFTA and how many jobs such exports might create in rural Mexico. Mexico in 1990 exported fruits and vegetables worth $900 million to the United States. Mexican agriculture official Luis Tellez has predicted that produce exports might reach $1.3 billion by 1998. How many jobs might an additional $400 million worth of produce exports create? Probably no more than 150,000: Mexico exported tomatoes worth $428 million in 1990, and tomato production created jobs from January through May for about 150,000 Mexican workers, suggesting that each $2,850 in tomato exports created one five-month seasonal job in Mexico.

It should be emphasized that jobs can be created in rural Mexico without increasing produce exports to the United States because rising Mexican incomes should increase Mexican consumption of fruits and vegetables. Mexico is already a major market for such commodities: about 82 percent of the fruits and vegetables produced in Mexico are consumed there. Since Mexicans consume more fresh vegetables than Americans, a NAFTA that stimulates economic growth should also create jobs to grow produce for Mexicans.

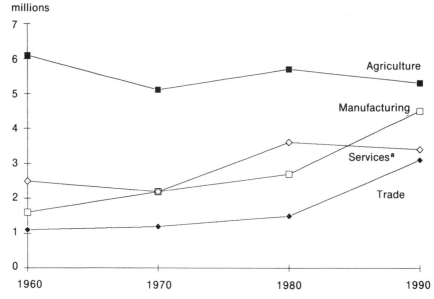

Figure 7 Mexico: employment by industry, 1960–90

a. Includes transportation and communications, community services, and financial services in 1980 and 1990.

Source: Mexican Census Bureau.

The Urban Mexican Labor Market

Ejido reforms, farm policy changes, and NAFTA promise to accelerate the pace of labor-displacing changes in rural Mexico. Those displaced in rural Mexico might be able to find jobs in urban areas of the country. There has already been considerable rural-urban migration, but agriculture still employs more Mexican workers than any other economic sector (figure 7). Agricultural employment has remained in the 5 million to 6 million range since 1960, while manufacturing employment tripled to 4.5 million. Manufacturing, trade, and service jobs tend to be in urban areas, so the evolution of jobs and wages in these urban sectors in the 1990s is likely to influence whether rural Mexicans seek urban jobs in Mexico or migrate to the United States.

Rural Mexican families found that Mexico's urban labor markets began to close to rural migrants in 1982, when the country's economic crisis slowed GDP growth and cut wages. Per capita GDP fell by 5.4 percent between 1981 and 1991, with the sharpest drop in 1986 (table 7). Real manufacturing wages fell sharply in 1982 to three-fourths of their 1980 levels, and they also hit lows relative to 1980 between 1986 and 1988. The real value of Mexico's minimum wage in urban areas fell throughout the 1980s, so that by 1991, it was only 42 percent of its 1980 level.

Table 7 Mexico: selected economic indicators, 1984–91

	1984	1985	1986	1987	1988	1989	1990	1991
GDP growth (percentages)	3.6	2.6	−3.8	1.8	1.4	3.1	3.9	4.0
Per capita growth (percentages)	1.2	0.2	−5.9	−0.5	−0.8	0.9	1.6	2.0
Real average manufacturing wages (1980=100)	75.0	76.0	72.0	71.0	72.0	75.0	78.0	77.0
Year-to-year change (percentage)	−7	2	−6	0	1	5	4	4
Real urban minimum wages (1980=100)	72	71	65	62	54	51	45	42
Year-to-year change (percentage)	−6	−2	−9	−5	−12	−6	−10	−6
Urban unemployment (percentage)[a]	5.7	4.4	4.3	3.9	3.5	2.9	2.9	2.6

a. Unemployment in Mexico City, Guadalajara, and Monterrey. Mexico counts as unemployed only those who are separated from formal employment relationships.

Source: Economic Commission for Latin American Countries (CEPAL), 1992. 1991 data are preliminary.

Despite falling real wages, the unemployment rate in Mexican cities has been lower than the unemployment rates in rural America, where many rural Mexicans sought jobs. However, the Mexican unemployment rate includes only those workers who left formal employment. Since fewer than 10 million of Mexico's 24 million to 30 million workers are in formal employment relationships, urban Mexican unemployment rates of 2 to 4 percent do not suggest that rural Mexicans are behaving irrationally when they seek jobs in US areas with 8 to 15 percent unemployment rates.

Some rural Mexicans migrated to urban areas in Mexico and queued for formal-sector jobs because, once in a formal-sector employment relationship, workers enjoy a vast array of constitutionally mandated benefits and protection. There are several definitions of formal sector employment, one of which is whether a worker is covered by the Mexican Social Security Institute, or IMSS. In 1990 IMSS covered about 40 percent of the labor force.[4]

About two-thirds of the manufacturing labor force was in the IMSS, as were a majority of the employees in wholesale and retail trade, but only one-fifth of the construction workers and one-fourth of the labor force were employed in the "other" sector. However, 60 percent of the Mexican workers are self-employed, are unpaid family workers, or are otherwise not working for wages and salaries in the formal labor market, and many of these informal-sector workers would be available for "real" or formal-sector wage and salary jobs if they become available.

There is little prospect that Mexico can achieve economic growth fast enough to reduce urban un- and underemployment during the 1990s, absorb new work force entrants, and find jobs for those displaced in rural Mexico. Even the most optimistic scenarios project that Mexico will gain at most 100,000 new jobs annually because of NAFTA, not enough even for the rural Mexicans that will be displaced. With rural-urban networks clogged and networks linking immigrants to the United States strengthened by US immigration reforms, the stage is set for a short-term rise in Mexico-to-US migration.

---

4. The percentage of the 1990 labor force in the social security system ranged from less than 10 percent in agriculture to 85 percent in services such as teaching and other community services, transportation, and financial services.

6

Networks and Continuing Migration

As the previous two chapters have described, a continued demand-pull in the US labor market and rising supply-push pressures in rural Mexico provide the two battery poles that will generate Mexico-to-US migration. An added stimulus is a network—what demographers used to call "intervening variables": the US contacts, immigration policies, and transportation and communications networks that bring Mexicans to the United States.

The networks that link rural Mexico to the United States have been forged over decades (Massey et al. 1987). While Mexico allowed its rural areas to become dependent on the US labor market, the United States converted winding paths into freeways through which Mexicans could enter the United States. The Bracero program planted the seed, and it proved to be naive to expect that, after 1 million to 2 million Mexicans had gained experience working seasonally in the United States, they would stop coming simply because the United States ended the program through which such workers arrived legally.

It was well-known that there were strong Mexico-US migration networks in the early 1980s, but what was not appreciated was that the Immigration Reform and Control Act (IRCA) of 1986 would strengthen rather than weaken these networks. IRCA was supposed to close the back door through which rural Mexicans were illegally entering the United States and to enlist US employers in the immigration control effort by making them liable to receive fines and imprisonment if they knowingly hired unauthorized workers. But IRCA backfired because of massive fraud in the legalization program and flawed enforcement of employer sanctions. Consequently, IRCA unleashed a new wave of unauthorized immigration.

For rural Mexicans in the mid-1980s, IRCA and especially its special agricultural worker (SAW) legalization program must have seemed a godsend. The September 1985 earthquake in Mexico City destroyed jobs and homes there, and recovery was slowed by foreign debts, which limited Mexico's ability to borrow on international markets. Prices were climbing at a dizzying rate: inflation was 120 percent in 1986 and 160 percent in 1987.

Some rural Mexicans took advantage of the SAW program to come to the United States in 1987 and 1988, even though many others did not immediately appreciate how easy it was to apply. During the spring of 1987, even though inflation in Mexico was rising and the peso was falling, fewer Mexicans than usual came north for the early US harvests, such as the May 1987 strawberry harvest in Oregon. Farmers complained of labor shortages. There were false rumors circulating in rural Mexico that, under IRCA, illegal aliens apprehended in the United States could be jailed or forced into the US armed forces, and so the farmer-funded Alien Legalization for Agriculture (ALFA) sent representatives to Mexico to explain how to apply for SAW legalization and to take applications there.

ALFA reported that there were workers in Mexico who qualified for SAW legalization but had to rely on US employers' recognition of them for proof they had met the 90-day work requirement during 1985–86. In order to get such proof, ALFA recommended that Mexican workers be permitted to enter the United States and visit their past employers to obtain letters to attach to their SAW applications. Since these workers were poor and because US farmers were experiencing labor shortages, farmers asked that these probationary entrants be allowed to work during their visits. Congress acquiesced, ordering the INS to accept provisional SAW applications from aliens who arrived at US ports of entry and made credible claims that they had done qualifying farm work. In this manner, over 100,000 Mexicans received 90-day work and residence permits to enable them to obtain SAW documentation.

There are only about 6 million adult males in rural Mexico, and over one-sixth of them eventually applied for the SAW program,[1] claiming that they had worked in US agriculture as illegal aliens in 1985–86. The INS soon became aware of the widespread "coaching" of alleged Mexican farm workers in border areas, and it was disapproving 9 out of 10 port-of-entry applicants by the time the SAW program ended in 1988. However, the INS was unprepared for the large number of SAW applicants, and it approved many applications from workers whose claims were

---

1. A small but unknown number of SAW applicants were from urban Mexico.

invalid on their face. SAW applicants often reported, for example, that they picked tomatoes for 92 days for one employer, even though the tomato harvesting season where the employer was located lasted only 50 to 60 days. There were a nontrivial number of cases in which SAW applicants asserted that they climbed ladders to pick strawberries or picked cans of beans from trees ("Fraud Suspected in Farm Jobs Program," *National Journal*, 24 September 1988, 2 and 411). In one of many postmortems on the worker- and industry-specific SAW legalization program, Robert Suro of *The New York Times* described it as "one of the most extensive immigration frauds ever perpetrated against the US government" (reprinted in the *Sacramento Bee*, 12 November 1989, A1).

SAW legalization has made it easier rather than harder for rural Mexicans to find US jobs. Most rural Mexicans believe they can still find jobs in the United States: one survey of farmers in three Mexican emigration villages in 1988–89 found that almost two-thirds believed it was still possible to get a job in the United States without "papers" or the legal right to work in the United States, including 86 percent of the workers who had never been to the United States (Cornelius 1991, 12). In these rural communities, "out-migration breeds more out-migration—and residents there increasingly view their community as a temporary refuge from labor in the United States rather than an environment for work and investment" (Cornelius 1990, 21).

If IRCA inadvertently strengthened rather than weakened the networks which bring Mexicans to the United States, the Immigration Act of 1990 deliberately strengthened them by expediting family unification and sending very mixed signals about whether the families of SAWs must wait in the family unification queue to join their relatives in the United States. The 1 million approved SAWs were mostly married Mexican men. Congress explicitly did not include their family members in the legalization program. However, family fairness and the other "gray-area" legal statuses that have evolved in recent years have encouraged some SAWs to bring their families to the United States (box 9). Under the family fairness policy, unauthorized family members of legalized aliens may remain in the United States and receive work authorization if they were here before 5 May 1988. Since the entry date for these family members is hard to disprove, some SAWs believe that even family members who arrived after this date will not be deported.

Remittances and the Culture of Emigration

A culture of emigration has evolved over decades in much of rural Mexico. In picturesque but poor villages, typically large (five-to seven-member) rural families have diversified their sources of income, and migration to the United States is an important part of their income-

Box 9   Family fairness and other side-door legal categories

In addition to the three mutually exclusive categories of aliens—immigrants, nonimmigrants, and unauthorized immigrants—there has been a recent proliferation of "side-door" immigration categories. Three of the most important are family unity, "persons permanently residing in the United States under color of law" (PRUCOL), and temporary protected status (TPS).

Family unity grants the most rights to gray-area aliens. Many of the illegal aliens who received legal immigrant status under 1987–88 legalization programs had family members who did not qualify. After five years as temporary US residents, these newly legalized aliens can petition to bring their families to the United States. Two-thirds of those legalized were from Mexico, and the wait for an immigrant visa for a wife or child can be two to three years. As a result, many newly legalized aliens brought their families illegally to the United States.

The spouses and children of most newly legalized aliens are expected to eventually be granted legal immigrant status. However, by coming illegally, families risk having some members deported. Therefore, a family fairness policy was written into the Immigration Act of 1990 that prevents the deportation of illegal spouses and children of newly legalized aliens, if they were in the United States before 5 May 1988. Family fairness rules permit otherwise illegal aliens to live and work legally in the United States until they reach the head of the visa queue. The number of aliens who have applied for family fairness status is relatively small, and some believe that families tend to apply only if the INS has located them.

TPS permits aliens to remain and work in the United States if their return is hampered by armed conflict or natural disaster. TPS is the status that was granted to certain El Salvadorans, Liberians, and Somalis during civil wars in their countries. TPS status can be revoked when conflicts at home end— TPS has been revoked for Lebanese and Kuwaitis. TPS for El Salvadorans ended on 30 June 1992, but they were granted a new status, "deferred enforced departure," which provides the same right to stay in the United States that TPS does.

PRUCOL is the broadest side-door legal status. This catchall category evolved in the mid-1970s, when Congress wanted to extend benefits to certain aliens but not put them into refugee or immigrant categories. PRUCOL is not defined in US immigration law; instead, PRUCOL is often defined by programs from which PRUCOL aliens seek benefits. For example, PRUCOL aliens living in the United States with INS knowledge and without the threat of deportation are generally eligible for Medicaid benefits but not Aid to Families with Dependent Children. A PRUCOL case might arise if, for example, an illegal-alien family with sick children is allowed to remain in the United States until the children are well.

The proliferation of in-between legal categories gives many aliens hope that, even if they are illegally in the US, they will be permitted to remain. Aliens who do not want to wait in immigration queues thus feel emboldened to come illegally. Each side-door status confers different access to social services and eventual US immigrant status.

earning portfolio. The two to four workers in each family may be deployed so that the mother stays in the village to farm the family's *ejido* land, the father and oldest son migrate to the United States, and the daughter seeks an urban services job (Taylor and Wyatt 1992; Taylor 1987). These dispersed families send home remittances throughout the year, and they often return in December and January for the fiesta season.

Remittances are a major source of foreign currency for the Mexican economy, and they are the lifeblood of many rural villages. In 1990, remittances were estimated to be $3.2 billion (Ascencio 1993, 64), equivalent to 1.5 percent of Mexican GDP, and more than both agricultural exports ($2.2 billion) and foreign direct investment ($2.6 billion). Mexican workers remit 20 to 40 percent of their US earnings, and the average $300 monthly that they send home can quadruple the income of a family with a worker in the United States—from the average $900 in rural Mexico to $3,600 or more (box 10).

In some rural villages, a majority of the adults are employed in the United States or in urban Mexico (Alarcon 1992). Remittances may be one-fourth to three-fourths of a village's total income, and the spending they make possible accounts for much of local economic activity, such as building new or improved housing for families of US migrant workers.

Since NAFTA is not likely to curb migration, remittances should continue to have important multiplier effects on rural Mexico's economy. If Mexico also changes its farm policies to substitute income transfers for price guarantees, then in most of rural Mexico, people might become dependent on externally generated funds. It is not clear what effect such an external lifeline would have on migration: it is possible that more Mexicans might live by the adage now common in emigration villages—"work in the United States but live in Mexico," emphasizing that enjoyment at home is the reward for work abroad.

Could Mexican rural development policies and NAFTA reverse this culture of emigration and an economy suited to it? Some hope that there will be a switch from corn to vegetable production, rooting more Mexicans to the land. But attitudes and economics work against any large-scale creation of jobs in this manner. Surveys in emigration villages find that many rural Mexicans have given up on agriculture—only 12 percent of 800 Mexican farmers surveyed in 1988–89 thought that agricultural improvements such as irrigation systems were their community's most important need versus more than twice this percentage who wanted factories to come to their villages and 37 percent who just wanted jobs (Cornelius 1991, 13). These emigration villages are often located too far from highways and railroads to justify locating factories in them, and those left behind after young workers are sent off to distant labor markets are not necessarily an attractive work force for potential factory operators.

Neither rural development nor NAFTA is likely to bring job-creating investments to these rural communities. A rural development strategy

Box 10   Remittances, development, and NAFTA

Remittances play a key role in rural Mexico's economic development, which in turn affects how many Mexican migrants will seek jobs in the United States in the 1990s. Migrant workers transfer remittances home both through formal banking channels and through informal channels such as carrying their cash savings home. The availability of remittances makes Mexican farmers less vulnerable to NAFTA-inspired changes in farm prices. However, any decrease in future migration and remittances may also have negative multiplier effects on economic activity in rural Mexico, spurring more migration.

Remittances to Mexico in the United States are estimated to be $2 billion to $6 billion annually. A recent study estimated that remittances in 1990 were $3.2 billion, equivalent to 1.5 percent of Mexico's GDP. About three-fourths of these remittances went to Mexico through formal banking channels, especially money orders.[1]

Most Mexican migrants come from central highlands states such as Michoacan, Jalisco, Guanajuato, Guerrero, and Zacatecas. In these states, remittances typically approach the federal government's public investment in the state. For example, in Michoacan in 1990, formal remittances were estimated to be $309 million, and federal public investment $361 million (Ascencio 1993, 67).

Remittances are more important as a source of foreign exchange than is foreign direct investment, suggesting their importance to the Mexican macroeconomy, but they are even more important to the villages in which the families who receive them live. Taylor (1993) surveyed 55 households in two agricultural villages four hours west of Mexico City in 1983 and 1989. One village relied on US remittances for 25 percent of the village's total income in 1982, and the other relied on US remittances for 13 percent of village income. By 1988, remittances as a share of village income fell to 20 percent in the first village and rose slightly to 14 percent in the second. Crop farming contributed less than 20 percent of total village income in 1982 and about 10 percent in 1989.

may be able to create micro-industries that encourage some potential migrants to stay at home. But the most likely prospect is for new jobs to be created in places far removed from the emigration areas so that young people will continue to migrate to find jobs. The question is whether they will stay in Mexico, perhaps by finding NAFTA-created jobs in Mexican factories or fields, or follow where their networks lead in the United States.

The declining importance of local farming income suggests that a NAFTA that makes farming less profitable will not necessarily lead to a large rise in US-bound migration. Taylor's data suggest that farmers in these villages have already diversified their sources of income, and village income increased during the 1980s as farmers invested their remittances in livestock and were able to sell the meat to urban consumers.

Taylor's data also suggest that migration and remittances promoted a shift from labor-intensive crop farming to livestock agriculture. Livestock have several advantages for migrant families. Remittances can be invested in them, solving the problem of where to invest. Also, women and children, who may not be able to produce crops, can care for livestock.

In villages surveyed by Taylor, livestock made both remittances and crop farming less important sources of income for the village. What will NAFTA do to these livestock-dependent villages? By lowering corn and bean prices, NAFTA should encourage even more investment in livestock, since their feed gets cheaper and the return for crops falls.

However, NAFTA might also encourage livestock agriculture to shift closer to the US border to take advantage of low-cost animal feed from the American Midwest. In that case, the income diversification that now seems to shelter some Mexican farmers from a decline in corn prices may nonetheless encourage emigration if NAFTA makes some current livestock agriculture less profitable.

---

1. In 1991 Banco de Mexico reported that 4.7 million money orders, each for an average $259, were sent from the United States to Mexico. There were also 1.6 million telegraph transfers for an average $333, and 257,000 personal checks. Electronic fund transfers, which cost the sender $25 each, were not included, although in one sample they averaged $676 each (Ascencio 1993, 29–31).

7

Maquiladoras and Stepping-Stone Migration

Displaced Mexican farmers in the 1990s may find jobs in factories and on farms created by the foreign investment that is expected to flow into Mexico as a result of Mexican policy reforms and the North American Free Trade Agreement (NAFTA). If such investment creates jobs, many are likely to be in labor-intensive and export-oriented operations in northern states of Mexico. Under this scenario, displaced rural Mexicans would have to migrate in the direction of the United States to find jobs. The question is, would new jobs in northern Mexico stop Mexicans from migrating to the United States, or would Mexicans use them as a stepping stone across the border?

No one knows exactly what kind of jobs NAFTA will create in Mexico, but there is a great deal of speculation that many of them will be like those created in maquiladoras. Maquiladoras are in-bond plants that turn imported components into finished goods that are typically reexported from Mexico. Mexico launched the maquiladora industry in 1965 in response to the unilateral US decision to terminate the Bracero program and in the hope that maquiladoras could provide year-round employment, financed by US investors, for Mexican workers who had become dependent on the US labor market. Many had moved their families to Mexican border cities, stimulating population growth there.

The number of maquiladoras and maquiladora jobs almost quadrupled during the 1980s, when legal and illegal Mexico-to-US migration also surged. This section investigates a seemingly simple question: what is the relationship between maquiladoras and migration, and what lessons does this experience hold for Mexico-to-US migration during the 1990s?

Box 11 The Mexican-American border

The Mexican-American border stretches for 2,000 miles, forming the southern boundaries of California, Arizona, New Mexico, and Texas. The border area is among the fastest-growing in both countries: some 3.5 million Mexicans and 4.6 million Americans live within 50 miles of the border, most in twin cities such as San Diego (2.5 million) and Tijuana (750,000).

Border cities	Population 1990 (thousands)
Tijuana, Baja California	743
San Diego, California	2,498
Mexicali, Baja California	602
Calexico, California	109
S. Luis Rio Colorado, Sonora	112
Yuma, Arizona	107
Nogales, Sonora	107
Nogales, Arizona	30
Agua Prieta, Sonora	39
Douglas, Arizona	98
Ciudad Juarez, Chihuahua	798
El Paso, Texas	592
Ciudad Acuna, Coahuila	57
Del Rio, Texas	139
Piedras Negras, Coahuila	98
Eagle Pass, Texas	36
Nuevo Laredo, Tamaulipas	219
Laredo, Texas	133
Reynosa, Tamaulipas	377
McAllen, Texas	384
Matamoros, Tamaulipas	303
Brownsville, Texas	260

Almost 200 million people cross the border legally each year, and another 2 million to 4 million cross it illegally.

Most of the border area is a desert. The border area population began to grow rapidly after 1965, when maquiladoras were permitted. The doubling

There seem to be five major points of agreement concerning maquiladoras:

- They have stimulated population and economic growth along the border. About 12 million people live within 50 miles of the US-Mexican border, one of the richest parts of Mexico and one of the poorest parts of the United States (box 11).

- They have not achieved their original goal—that is, to provide jobs for ex-Bracero men who had become dependent on the US labor market.

of maquiladora plants (to 2,000) and employment (to 500,000) during the 1980s helps to explain why the border-area population rose over 70 percent during the decade. Much of this population growth occurred on the Mexican side of the border, which is one of the richest regions of Mexico. On the US side, population growth was fueled by immigration from Mexico, as well as retirement, military, and maquiladora activities.[1] The poverty that marks the US side of the border has led some to describe it as the Third-World part of the United States: three-quarters of all families had incomes in 1990 below the poverty line of $13,359 for a family of four. In Texas and New Mexico, many of these poor families live in *colonias,* areas in which lots without water and electricity connections are sold.

How will NAFTA affect border-area economies and environments? There are two opposing views. One view is that, after NAFTA, maquiladora operations will move further inside Mexico to cities such as Monterrey, which is three hours from the border. Moving maquiladoras inland should decrease migration to the border area, thus reducing the strain on the border area's environment, as well as stepping-stone migration to the United States, and raise the percentage of Mexican-supplied inputs used in maquiladora operations.[2] Maquiladora managers would also move to Mexico.

The other argument is that NAFTA will simply accelerate border-area maquiladora development. This argument notes that operations just inside the Mexican border can gain access to low-cost Mexican labor and take maximum advantage of US infrastructure. Foreign investors, some argue, prefer to deal with American-oriented Mexicans in the border region and thus will continue to locate there unless environmental or some other tax or policy instruments push them inland.

---

1. The managers of maquiladora factories in Mexico typically live in the United States, where their warehousing operations are. Maquiladora workers promote growth on the US side by spending, by one estimate, 40 to 60 percent of their wages on what are perceived to be higher-quality American goods, explaining the large number of shopping centers on the US side of the border (*The Economist*, 12 December 1992, 22).

2. Border-area maquiladoras use an average 2 percent Mexican-produced inputs, while Monterrey maquiladoras use 30 percent local inputs.

- They employ primarily young women at the Mexican minimum wage. Rather than raising wages, employers tolerate high turnover and compete for workers by offering noncash benefits.

- Maquiladoras are changing. Many are hiring more men, moving to interior locations, and producing more sophisticated products with better-educated workers.

- NAFTA will eventually eliminate maquiladoras in the present sense.

There is no agreement, however, over the maquiladora-migration relationship. Two extreme assertions frame the debate: some argue that there is no relationship (Huerta 1990b), others find that Oaxacan workers recruited for seasonal farm jobs in Baja California used this internal Mexican migration as a stepping stone into the United States (Zabin et al. 1993).

A middle position is that "the maquiladora industry is now a positive attraction for [internal Mexican] migrants" and that, even though most internal Mexican migrants hope to stay in Mexico, "a decline or slowdown in maquiladora job creation" could lead to border-city unemployment and cross-border migration (Brannon and Lucker 1988, 30). Other analyses of maquiladoras reach similar conclusions (Stoddard 1987; Sklair 1989; Weintraub 1990).

Caution suggests that new NAFTA-induced investments in Mexico should be steered away from the border area. In this way, any stimulus to cross-border migration is discouraged, Mexico's interior infrastructure can be upgraded faster, and there is less need to further strain the border-area infrastructure.

The Maquiladora System

The maquiladora system is fairly transparent. Foreign components and any machinery needed to assemble them are imported duty-free into Mexico, goods are processed or assembled there, and then the finished goods are reexported, usually to the United States. As the finished goods enter the United States, the US tariff schedule limits duties on them to the value that was added by Mexican assembly operations. Two industries—autos and auto parts, and electronics—account for a majority of maquiladora employment, so a typical maquiladora would import US-made television parts, assemble them into televisions, and then export the televisions to the United States.[1] US duty is paid only on the cost of the Mexican labor and plant operations, which are typically 10 to 30 percent of US assembly costs.

The value added by Mexican inputs and assembly operations is small; about 20 percent of the value of finished maquiladora goods. Almost all the Mexican value added comes from Mexican wages and plant opera-

1. Most of the televisions sold in the United States are assembled in Mexico in US- and Japanese-owned plants. If Japanese-made parts are used, they are often imported into the United States, where a duty is paid on them, and then sent to Mexico.

In March 1993 the cost of a 19-inch Sony television assembled in Mexico was $245; imported components were $219 or 89 percent of these costs. Sony Mexico expects NAFTA to primarily affect its ability to compete in the Mexican market. By removing tariffs on North American components, the cost of imported components such as picture tubes is expected to fall by 40 percent, eliminating the current situation in which televisions assembled in Mexico cost more there than in the United States (interview with J. Luis Zuñiga, Tijuana, March 1993).

tions: half comes from the wages and salaries paid to workers, and another 45 percent comes from utilities and other business expenses. Only 1 to 2 percent represents Mexican-produced components (Weintraub 1990, 4).

Maquiladoras have enjoyed explosive growth. There were 12 maquiladoras employing 3,000 workers in 1965, 120 employing 20,300 workers in 1970, and almost 600 employing 120,000 workers in 1980 (table 8). Between 1985 and 1990, the number of maquiladoras more than doubled, from 800 to 1,900, and maquiladora employment rose from 212,000 to 472,000.[2] In 1988 maquiladora employment of 369,000 was reported to be 15.5 percent of Mexican manufacturing employment and 1.5 percent of total Mexican employment.[3] If maquiladora employment doubles again every five years in the 1990s, then by 2000 there would be almost 2 million Mexicans employed in maquiladoras.

Maquiladoras provide jobs, wages, and export earnings. Wages and benefits totaling $1.8 billion for an average 472,000 workers in 1990 suggest that workers had average annual earnings of about $3,800, well above Mexico's $2,300 per capita income. If the average maquiladora worker is a member of a family of five (Weintraub 1990, 4), then maquiladora employment contributes to the income of almost 2.5 million people, or 3 percent of Mexico's population. Each maquiladora job creates, by some estimates, two to three additional jobs, so 500,000 maquiladora jobs may be responsible for 1 million to 1.5 million additional service, housing, and related jobs.

Maquiladoras loom large in the labor market and in Mexico's trade picture. Maquiladora "exports" are included in trade data as nonfactor services, so their value added is recorded in the national accounts in the same way that tourist spending in Mexico is. Maquiladoras raised their

---

2. In 1990 there were 348 plants with 103,500 employees in electronics, 112 plants with 90,500 employees in autos, and 245 plants with 39,100 employees in textiles.

3. This implies a manufacturing work force of 2.4 million and a total work force of 23.1 million (Huerta 1990a, 74). It should be noted that data on Mexican manufacturing employment are in conflict. According to Mexican government surveys, Mexico's 137,200 manufacturing establishments employed 2.5 million workers in 1989, and 90 percent are wage and salary workers. The 750,000 wholesale and retail trade establishments employed 2 million workers, but only 54 percent are wage and salary workers. Nongovernment services employ 1.7 million workers, of whom two-thirds are wage and salary workers.

These data, from Banamex, disagree with estimates of Mexican manufacturing employment made by the US Department of Labor based on 1986 International Labor Organization data: they put the 472,000 maquiladora employees at 11 percent of Mexico's manufacturing employment, implying 4.3 million manufacturing workers. An ILO study reported 587,000 manufacturing employees in 1980, suggesting that maquiladora employment was 20 percent of total manufacturing employment in that year, but it was noted that "other sources give a considerably higher level of employment in Mexico's manufacturing industry" (Van Liemt 1988, 3).

Table 8. Mexico: maquiladora employment and exports: 1965–90

Year	Maquiladoras	Employment	Exports[a] (millions of dollars)	Exports (percentages)[b]	Wages and benefits paid (millions of dollars)
1965	12	3,000	n.a.	n.a.	n.a.
1970	120	20,327	83	6	n.a.
1975	454	67,213	332	11	194
1980	578	119,546	772	5	456
1985	789	211,968	1,268	6	540
1990	1,924	472,000	3,635	14	n.a.

n.a. = not available

a. Value added in Mexico. For example, in 1990, the difference in value between the components imported into Mexico and the value of maquiladora exports was $3.6 billion, or about 14 percent of Mexico's $26 billion merchandise exports.

b. Percent of Mexico's merchandise exports.

Source: Adapted from Hufbauer and Schott (1992, 92) and Huerta (1990a, 75).

value added from 4 percent of Mexico's merchandise exports in 1980 to 14 percent in 1990, when maquiladora value added was $3.6 billion.

Maquiladora operations were from the beginning attractive to foreign investors because of low Mexican wages, but maquiladora growth in the 1980s awaited declining Mexican wages. Hourly compensation in US dollars in Mexico's national manufacturing industries and in maquiladoras fell by almost 50 percent between 1980 and 1986–87, while wages in Asian export platform countries such as Korea continued their steady rise.

By the mid-1980s, maquiladora wages were lower than Asian wages, and this Mexican cost advantage continued to widen during the late 1980s. Maquiladora labor costs are considerably lower than labor costs in Mexico's non-maquiladora manufacturing sector; maquiladora labor costs average just 50 percent of the labor costs in large and sometimes government-owned factories in which most workers are represented by unions. However, wage comparisons between national industries and maquiladoras can be misleading, since national industries include, for example, the Pemex oil company, which has a unionized and mostly male work force, while maquiladoras include electronics assembly operations with mostly nonunion female work forces.

Maquiladora Employment

Maquiladoras are an emotional topic quite apart from their effects on illegal migration. They create jobs that pay above-average wages, and they generate foreign exchange. But they have fallen short in other areas: the presence of maquiladoras has generated relatively few jobs in Mexican supplier industries because the maquiladoras use few local components. There also seems to be little training provided to local workers, in part because of high worker turnover; the average tenure in the industry is less than 10 years.

Maquiladoras most often locate in industrial parks that house a variety of industries. The park manager arranges for water, electricity, and security, but the individual maquiladora managers determine wages, fringe benefits, and working hours and conditions. Mexican law requires managers to pay at least the minimum wage for the area and to provide some fringe benefits, but many managers provide more. Maquiladoras seem reluctant to compete on wages; entry-level wages are almost always the minimum for the area. Instead, maquiladoras tend to compete by tolerating high turnover rates and by offering additional noncash benefits.

Maquiladoras have been monopsonists in their local labor markets, facing an elastic supply of labor at the minimum wage. The plants initial preference for young women has been ascribed to their willingness to work for low wages, their dexterity, and their willingness to perform tedious and repetitive tasks; it was also argued that young women would be least receptive to unions (Brannon and Lucker 1988, 7–8). Young women have remarkably high labor force participation rates in border cities: in some cities, 60 to 80 percent of the 20- to 24-year-old women are in the work force.

Until the growth in maquiladora employment in the mid-1980s, managers could be selective about who they hired. They preferred young women who supposedly would not have been in the labor force if they were not employed in maquiladoras. Maquiladoras often refused to hire nonlocal workers; before 1985 there were queues of workers waiting to be hired at the better maquiladoras, and internal migrants had to find jobs for one or two years in plants that offered physically demanding work before they could land jobs at plants operated by well-known US multinationals.

As the labor market tightened after the mid-1980s, maquiladora managers responded in three ways. First, they began to hire previously excluded workers: men, recent migrants, and older women. Second, they adapted their production and hiring systems to high turnover and sought to retain employees by providing up to half of the total wage in a variety of fringe benefits. Third, some maquiladoras sought interior locations, where labor was more readily available.

Recent surveys of maquiladora workers suggest that there is a trend toward hiring men, providing training, and producing sophisticated products, but it is evolving very slowly. One of the largest worker surveys was conducted in 1988–89 by Mario M. Carillo Huerta (1990a) for the US Commission for the Study of International Migration and Cooperative Economic Development. Some 1,200 maquiladora workers were interviewed in the winter of 1988–89.[4] Half were migrants (born in another Mexican state), and half were local workers (born in the same state in which the maquiladora was located). The work force was very young: 45 percent were 15 to 19 years old, including 52 percent of the local workers (table 9). About 80 percent of the workers were not married, and 80 percent had an elementary school education or less. Almost 60 percent were in their first maquiladora job, and over half had received no training before going to work. The maquiladora work force profiled in these data is an unskilled and entry-level one.

Huerta's survey is indicative of previous surveys, which also report predominantly young and poorly educated workers who have been employed only a short time in the maquiladora near which they were interviewed. Like Huerta, earlier surveys reported that managers

---

4. The sample was drawn to reflect the total maquiladora work force, which was 38 percent men and 62 percent women. (Huerta 1990a, 13).

Table 9 Mexico: maquiladora work force characteristics, 1988–89
(percentages)

Worker characteristics	Percentages	Worker characteristics	Percentages
Age		Major reason for migration	
15–19	45	Seek a job	27
20–24	34	Accompany family	21
Not married	80	Seek a better life	14
Elementary education	80	Had maquila job offer	
In first maquiladora job	58	before migrating	10
No training received on the job	52	Other	28
Moved from urban area	72		
In area less than four years	51		

Based on a survey of 1,200 maquiladora workers conducted in December 1988–January 1989.

Source: Adapted from Huerta (1990a, 80–83).

intended to hire more men and to provide more training, but there is as yet only limited evidence that these intentions have been realized.

Most maquiladora workers are not represented by unions. Almost half of all maquiladora employment is in largely nonunion Juarez and Tijuana. Unionization declines from east to west along the US-Mexican border. The maquiladora work force in 1990 was practically 100 percent unionized in the easternmost border cities of Matamoros, Reynosa, and Nuevo Laredo but less than 30 percent unionized in the western border cities of Mexicali and Tijuana (Williams 1990, 3). Williams concluded that antiunion employers, backed by the federal government, have been able to discourage the unionization of young workers whose high turnover may limit their interest in unions.

Maquiladoras and Migration

The issue of whether maquiladoras act "as a magnet for the internal migration of Mexicans to the north of the country and internationally to the United States" has been investigated throughout the 1980s (Seligson and Williams 1981, 9). Most of the studies are based on interviews with maquiladora workers employed in border cities. Interviewers determined the workers' place of origin, satisfaction with maquiladora employment, and plans to migrate further. Most surveys (e.g., Huerta 1990a; Brannon and Lucker 1988; Stoddard 1981; Sklair 1989; Weintraub 1990; Zabin et al. 1993) found the following:

■ During the 1980s, more Mexicans began to migrate to the border in search of maquiladora employment, indicating that the migrant percentage of maquiladora work forces has been rising.

- At the time they were interviewed, few maquiladora workers had ever worked in the United States—legally or illegally—and few expressed an interest in using their maquiladora savings to finance illegal entry into the United States. Few thought that their maquiladora training would help them obtain a US factory job.

- However, there seems to be a small but rising amount of stepping-stone migration, perhaps attributable to the rising proportion of internal migrants and men in maquiladora work forces.

These surveys suggest that maquiladoras are not now but could become a trampoline that brings more Mexican workers to the United States, reinforcing environmental and infrastructural reasons to encourage job creation further from the border.

Most maquiladora-migration studies ask workers exiting industrial parks questions such as, "Have you ever worked in the United States?" Of Huerta's 1,200-worker sample, 11 percent answered yes. In response to the question, "Do you think that maquiladora employment will improve your chances of finding a US job?" 28 percent answered yes (Huerta 1990a, 24). Some interviewers in the Huerta study probed further, asking questions such as whether maquiladora workers prefer their current jobs (29 percent in Huerta) to a similar US job (21 percent) or a similar job in their place of origin (21 percent) or whether they have no preference about where they work (28 percent). Some 16 percent of the workers Huerta interviewed wanted to enter the United States illegally, and 41 percent indicated that, if they had legal status, they would prefer to live in the United States (Huerta 1990a, 25–26).

Huerta concluded that 84 percent of the maquiladora workers interviewed had no desire to emigrate at the time of the interview. She acknowledged that maquiladoras play an increasingly important role in drawing internal migrants to border areas, but she concluded that maquiladora employment discourages migration to the United States because "employment in the maquiladoras represents a much preferred option to employment in the United States" (Huerta 1990a, 27).

Surveys of the future intentions of maquiladora workers may suffer from the flaws common to surveys of immigrants, including farm workers. The median age of hired farm workers has been and remains young—in the 24- to 28-year-old range. When interviewed, most farm workers report that they expect to be doing farm work next year—they might prefer a year-round job, but most see little hope of getting one. But farm workers do get out of farm work: a constant median age in an industry with stable employment means that older workers are being replaced by young workers. Asking farm workers about their intentions would suggest that they never exit the work force; similarly, one might question the reliability of cross-section interview data on the intentions of maquiladora workers.

A direct link between maquiladoras and migration is hard to observe because of the contrasting profiles of maquiladora workers and migrants: the maquiladora workers are mostly young women, while US-bound migrants tend to be young men. Interviews with currently employed maquiladora women say little about the migration behavior of young men, since men and women tend to be found in equal proportions in most areas, maquiladoras might indirectly encourage US migration by drawing men to border areas. These men may use border cities only as a staging area, and thus never intend to have a maquiladora career, but they know that the economic activity stimulated by maquiladoras can provide them with informal employment while they are waiting to cross the border.

Some migration researchers emphasize that US-Mexican migration networks are so well-developed that migrants do not need to engage in two-stage migration; they can migrate directly to the United States. For example, surveys in three interior Mexican communities with varying emigration histories found that about one-fourth of the adults were considering a permanent move. Among these potential emigrants, three-fourths planned a US destination and one-fourth a Mexican destination. From this, researchers deduced that those planning long-distance moves preferred the United States to Mexico for its much higher wages, and their US contacts were sufficient to make this option realistic (Cornelius 1990, 29). Only 7 percent of the potential movers were considering a move to a Mexican border city, which suggested to the researchers that the booming maquiladora industry was *not* attracting migrants from areas that traditionally sent migrants to the United States. Other research that suggests no relationship between maquiladoras and migration includes Seligson and Williams (1981), Sklair (1989), Brannon and Lucker (1988), and Dávila and Saenz (1990).

If maquiladora or similar factory employment were to double again due to NAFTA-stimulated foreign investment, this expansion by itself is not likely to double illegal Mexico-to-US entries. The relationship between the growth of maquiladoras and illegal US migration is closer to 0 than to 1, but it is slightly positive, tending to increase, and probably most important in its hard-to-measure indirect effects. For these reasons, it would be better to encourage the creation of maquiladoras, where possible, further from the border. However, it is better to have a border-area factory jobs than no jobs: as the Mexican adage goes, it is better to be "exploited" in a maquiladora or in a US job than to not be exploited at all.

Export-Oriented Agriculture

Maquiladoras do not prove a "smoking gun" link between border-area factory jobs and illegal US migration. But Mexico's winter vegetable

industry does: the expansion of the industry, especially in Baja California, is widely credited with introducing indigenous peoples from southern Mexico into the United States in the late 1980s (Zabin et al. 1993).
In the case of agriculture, it appears that the creation of seasonal jobs
closer to the US border did, in this case, encourage stepping-stone migration across the border.

Mexico's export-oriented vegetable industry is centered in Sinaloa,
about 600 miles south of the US border. Large farms there employ about
170,000 Mexican workers for four to five months. Most of these seasonal
workers are migrants: three-fourths migrate to Sinaloa from other parts
of Mexico, and seasonal work there ends there just as US growers begin
to hire farm workers.

The Sinaloa fresh vegetable industry developed in the 1950s after the
Mexican government constructed dams to provide irrigation water and
paved a highway to the US border. US growers and distributors formed
partnerships with local growers to produce for the US market. After the
United States embargoed trade with Cuba in 1960, Sinaloa production
expanded so that by 1969 Sinaloa was providing 75 percent of the fresh
tomatoes consumed in the United States during the winter months.
However, Florida producers resisted Mexican imports with tariff and
nontariff barriers and technological advances and have maintained a
two-thirds share of the US winter fresh vegetable market since the early
1980s, the same share Mexican producers held in the mid-1970s.

Tomatoes are about 30 percent of the value of the $900 million worth
of fruits and vegetables that Mexico exported to the United States in
1990. Tomatoes are picked in the United States and in Mexico largely
by migrant Mexican workers. The Mexican migrants in Florida tend to
be young men without their families, while the Mexican migrants in
Sinaloa include far more families. Wages are higher in Florida: workers
average $5 to $6 hourly, and although the hours of work they can obtain
fluctuates between 25 and 45 weekly, most expect to earn $3,000 to
$4,000 for 20 weeks of tomato picking. In Mexico, workers average $6
to $8 daily and $500 to $800 per season, but lax enforcement of child
labor laws means that in many cases entire families work, narrowing
the household earnings gap. The income gap is further reduced by the
frequent provision of free housing for migrant workers in Mexico, and its
usual absence in Florida. Despite housing and transportation expenses,
young men can earn more in Florida. For families who in any event
might have a more difficult time crossing the border illegally, the earnings
gap is much narrower.

Surveys of workers employed in Mexico's winter vegetable industry
during the 1980s echoed maquiladora studies in finding that a growing
percentage of the workers were migrants. A survey in 1974 found that
56 percent of 180,000 peak seasonal workers were migrants. By 1985 an

estimated 80 percent of 170,000 peak workers were migrants, and the sharpest jump was in the share of long-distance or interstate migrants, whose share of the work force rose from 25 to 75 percent (Thompson and Martin 1989, 14). As with maquiladora workers, Mexican migrants in Sinaloa were asked about their migration intentions, and 27 percent in 1985 intended to continue migrating north to Baja California or the United States. These continuing migrants tended to be single, young, and landless men; migrant families with small farms were more likely to return to them.

Seasonal work in northern Mexican border states appears to have led to a renewed cross-border migration network. The United States probably has most of North America's migrant farm workers—about 800,000, versus 400,000 in Mexico and 20,000 to 30,000 in Canada. Migrant farm workers who are US citizens traditionally have shuttled between winter homes in southern Florida, Texas, and California-Arizona, and summer jobs in the northern US states. However, the aging of the migrant work force, the availability of unemployment insurance and other government services in their homes in southern states, and the destruction of housing for migrant families in northern US states have since the late 1980s substituted solo Mexican men who shuttle from Mexico and into the US Midwest and Northeast for the previous interstate US migration of families. The newest of these Mexican shuttle workers appear to be the southern Mexicans initially recruited to work in northern Mexico.

Although researchers of maquiladoras found no such connection, the expansion of commercial agriculture in Baja California's San Quintin Valley provides a clear example of stepping-stone migration from southern Mexico to the United States. The 10 growers who farm there use US capital and seeds to produce tomatoes and other vegetables for the US and Mexican markets. Several farm 1,000 to 4,000 acres, making them large employers even by US standards, with peak migrant work forces of 2,000 or more. Most of the migrant workers they employ are Mixtec Indians from the southern Mexican state of Oaxaca.

Yet there are believed to be more Mixtecs employed in California agriculture than in Baja California agriculture: they are two-thirds of the 35,000-peak workers in Baja and almost 10 percent of the peak of 450,000 farm workers in California. Surveys of these Mixtec workers in California and Oregon reveal that two-thirds had worked in Baja California, and that, while there, US foremen, labor contractors, and friends and relatives encouraged them to seek US jobs (Zabin et al. 1993). Like maquiladora managers, Baja California growers have adapted to the turnover of Mixtec workers that they recruit in southern Mexico: some report that two of three workers brought by bus to Baja California in northern Mexico migrate on to the United States before the end of the harvest season, prompting the growers to "over-recruit."

If export-oriented agriculture expands in Northern Mexico, there is likely to be more internal Mexican migration for seasonal jobs that in turn could fuel migration across the border. The relationship between maquiladoras and migration may be unclear, but the relationship between export-oriented Mexican agriculture, internal migration, and Mexico-to-US migration is clearer: bringing Mexicans closer to the border in this case also encourages cross-border migration.

Steering Investment in Mexico

There are about 500,000 maquiladora jobs and 200,000 seasonal farm worker jobs in Mexico that produce for the US market; both numbers are likely to rise once NAFTA is in place. New jobs created in border areas and filled by internal Mexican migrants may increase the likelihood of stepping-stone migration to the United States.

Probabilities for stepping-stone migration should not be used as excuses to slow the implementation of NAFTA. However, to the extent that the US and Mexican governments can influence where new jobs are created in Mexico, they should promote interior rather than border job creation. Especially in the agricultural sector, there appears to be far less stepping-stone migration from Sinaloa, 600 miles from the US border, than from Baja California, 60 miles from the border.

Coping with Migration

8

Conclusions

Presidents Bush and Salinas embraced the North American Free Trade Agreement (NAFTA) as a means for accelerating economic growth in both countries by encouraging each to specialize in those goods in which it has a comparative advantage and then to trade these goods without border barriers. For most of the 20th century, one of Mexico's comparative advantages in the North American economy has been in unskilled workers. NAFTA, it is hoped, can substitute labor-intensive goods and services exports for the export of people from Mexico and eventually reduce Mexican migration to the United States. Economic growth and development, accelerated by free trade and investment, is a proven strategy for stopping unwanted migration.

Postwar Europe is often cited as an instance where this strategy worked. After World War II, economic integration in Europe occurred with free trade and without significant migration between the North Atlantic economies. Within Western Europe, northern and southern economies were integrated after a migration hump that peaked in the 1960s and early 1970s. These experiences may be only partially applicable to North American economic integration. This is because today's economic gaps between the United States and Mexico are larger than the gaps between the North Atlantic and Western European economies in the 1950s, North American labor markets are far more closely linked at the outset of the integration process than were labor markets in northern and southern Europe, and the US immigration control system is less effective at controlling unauthorized entries than were northern European systems.

NAFTA will test how free trade and investment affects an ongoing migration relationship characterized by labor market interdependence and large economic gaps between countries. But it will not be a pure test because Mexico has already unilaterally adopted policies that opened its economy and reforms that will promote long-run growth but tend to drain people from the countryside. Simultaneously, the United States, with its easy legalization programs and ineffective enforcement of immigration laws during the 1980s, made it easier rather than harder for Mexicans to work in the United States.

NAFTA is likely to affect migration. But this important issue did not take center stage during the negotiations, and analysts are forced to perform a two-stage analysis—first projecting the effects of the agreement on economic variables and then speculating about how potential migrants might respond to these economic changes. It is hard enough to get consensus on how free trade is likely to affect exports and imports, and thus jobs and wages, in each country; it is harder still to project how potential migrants are likely to respond.

Analyses of NAFTA's potential effect on migration tend to fall at two extremes. At the one extreme are those who argue that NAFTA will begin to reduce emigration the moment the agreement is signed. This seems to be the attitude of US political leaders and NAFTA negotiators— migration is occurring, but a signed NAFTA raises hopes for economic betterment in Mexico, setting the stage for gradually diminishing the flow so that this controversial topic need not be addressed in order to approve NAFTA. Migration, in this view, will gradually diminish as NAFTA takes effect.

At the other extreme are analysts who begin with the fact that Mexico has 2 million to 3 million farmers who are more or less dependent on producing corn, a crop in which Mexico does not have a comparative advantage. Their migration scenarios begin with projections of how freer trade in corn and other farm products is likely to displace rural Mexicans, some of whom would undoubtedly migrate to the United States. One recommendation of these studies is to slow implementation of free trade in farm commodities such as corn, under the theory that what is good for Iowa corn exporters is bad for Los Angeles job seekers and social service providers.

This study takes a different tack. It begins with the three major variables that determine the flow of Mexico-to-US migrants—demand-pull in the United States, supply-push in Mexico, and networks and a culture of emigration in rural Mexico—and then examines how NAFTA is likely to affect each. The conclusion is that NAFTA affects all three factors in a manner that temporarily increases Mexico-to-US migration. This migration hump should not be ignored, nor should it be an excuse to stall NAFTA. Despite the migration hump, there will be less Mexico-to-

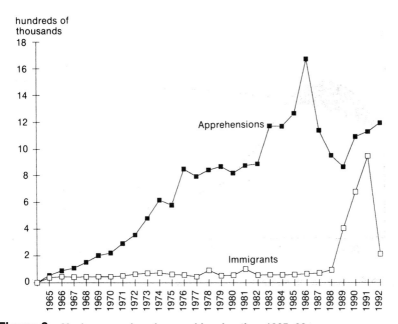

Figure 8 Mexico: apprehensions and immigration, 1965–92

Source: Immigration and Naturalization Service, *Statistical Yearbook*, annual.

US migration over the next two decades with NAFTA than without NAFTA. For this reason, NAFTA should be implemented as planned in order to lay the basis for stay-at-home development in Mexico.

Figure 8 compares Mexican apprehensions and legal immigration between 1965 and 1992. Apprehensions rose steadily throughout the late 1960s and early 1970s, then leveled off in the late-1970s before beginning to climb sharply after 1982. Apprehensions peaked in 1986, and after falling to 850,000 in 1989, have resumed their upward climb. Legal immigration only partially mirrors apprehensions. There were an average 55,000 legal Mexican immigrants annually between 1965 and 1980, but an average 235,000 between 1981 and 1992. Total Mexico-to-US immigration—legal and illegal—has been on an upward trend.

Between 1994 and 2010, there will be less Mexico-to-US migration with NAFTA than without NAFTA (figure 9). Two points deserve emphasis. First, NAFTA is likely to add relatively little to what is already a significant flow of Mexicans to the United States—on the order of 10 percent to a flow of 200,000 to 300,000 legal and illegal Mexican immigrants annually. Second, NAFTA reduces Mexican immigration when viewed from 2010: the migration hump should be a short-lived phenomenon. Seen in this light, NAFTA is a very worthwhile investment for the United States to make in order to eventually reduce unwanted Mexican immigration.

The NAFTA migration hump has become conventional wisdom for both opponents and proponents. Some proponents argue that without

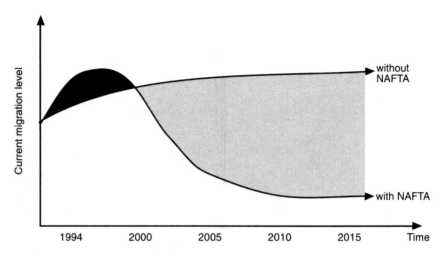

Figure 9 Mexico-US migration with and without NAFTA: a qualitative projection.

NAFTA, the migration hump will be larger. For example, it has been speculated that, if NAFTA is not approved, there may be 500,000 additional illegal Mexican immigrants annually (*Wall Street Journal*, 28 May 1993, A7). Such estimates are highly speculative: there is little evidence they are based on emigration intentions in the traditional or more recent sending regions of Mexico and they cannot assess the extent to which potential migrants are remaining in Mexico in the hope that NAFTA will soon bring them jobs. Emigration pressures from Turkey did not increase sharply when the European Community rebuffed Turkey's application in 1989, and the argument that without NAFTA there will be a migration hump traceable to disappointment in Mexico rests on, at best, very anecdotal evidence. Dismissing the speculation that potential US-bound migrants are waiting to see if NAFTA will be ratified, there will not be a migration hump if the agreement is rejected, and there will be no quick diminution of the flow if NAFTA is approved.

There is no real basis for attaching numbers to projected immigration from Mexico. In 1981, when there were 100,000 legal Mexican immigrants and 900,000 illegal Mexicans apprehended in the United States, there were no projections that a decade later there would be over 900,000 legal Mexican immigrants and 1.1 million apprehensions. The number of legal Mexican immigrants has fluctuated with US policy changes, but the overall flow of legal and illegal immigrants combined is rising.

NAFTA's likely effect on rural Mexican emigration can be framed by two extreme views of how dependent potential migrants there are on Mexican government subsidies and institutional rules. At one extreme are modelers such as Hinojosa and McCleery (1992), Hinojosa and Robinson (1991b), and Calva (1992); they assume that many corn farmers are kept in rural Mexico by high prices, which will be reduced under NAFTA, and by a land tenure system that ties people to the land. At the other extreme are those who have observed these farmers (e.g., Taylor 1992); they emphasize that, in much of rural Mexico, farmers have already diversified the sources of their income, and that despite land tenure laws, *ejido* land is routinely rented and leased so that a NAFTA-inspired reduction in Mexican corn prices will affect, at most, only 20 to 40 percent of a typical rural household's income. In both cases, NAFTA adds to emigration pressure in rural Mexico. But in the modeling perspective, lower corn prices eliminate all or most of a rural family's income, while the empirical studies emphasize that reducing corn prices affects only a small fraction of the household's income. The data to determine which assumption is generally valid are not available.

NAFTA can be expected to increase Mexico-to-US migration, but only temporarily and only marginally compared with the current flow. Most demographers and economists expect legal immigration from Mexico to average 100,000 to 200,000 annually during the 1990s, but with a total influx that has been averaging 300,000, there are likely to be another 100,000 to 200,000 illegal settlers. If, for example, NAFTA increased the flow by 10 percent, the effect would be that an 11-year "normal" Mexican flow of immigrants would arrive within 10 years because of NAFTA. However, after 2000, the more rapid economic growth and job creation due to NAFTA should reduce the "normal" Mexican influx. Demographic factors will also dampen emigration pressures after 2000.

NAFTA will lead to a small migration hump, although precise estimations of its size are not possible, because it affects the three major migration variables in a manner that stimulates more migration, albeit only marginally. When migration is considered over two decades, there is less migration with NAFTA than without NAFTA. Consequently, this study concludes that a manageable migration hump is a reasonable price to pay for less unwanted Mexican immigration in the long run.

Must Migration Be Considered in NAFTA?

The debate over NAFTA has so far avoided extensive discussion of its migration consequences. There are several reasons, not the least of which is that those interested in migration know little about trade, and vice versa. Although immigration seems to be a growing political issue, especially in California, the costs that recent arrivals impose on state and local governments have so far only occasionally been linked to the debate over whether NAFTA should be ratified.

Those opposed to NAFTA seem to have found enough ammunition in fears of job losses and environmental degradation that they do not need to raise another reason. It might be risky for NAFTA opponents to reject the agreement on migration grounds: unions are often allies of civil rights and ethnic groups, which generally oppose more effective immigration controls. Both the Mexican American Legal Defense and Educational Fund (MALDEF) and the American Friends Service Committee (AFSC) took the position that the United States should recognize the Mexicans' growing presence and should accompany NAFTA with another amnesty and a moratorium on the enforcement of employer sanctions (testimony to the US Office of the Special Trade Representation, 9 September 1991).

Immigration control and environmental groups, on the other hand, could prove to be uncomfortable allies for unions in non-NAFTA matters. Immigration control groups would like to use the potential NAFTA migration hump to take the steps they think are necessary to control illegal immigration: a fraud-resistant identity document, stepped-up border enforcement, and a moratorium on immigration (Simcox 1991). Since some of these groups would embrace NAFTA if immigration control efforts were stepped up, they have not been welcomed into the anti-NAFTA fold.

If immigration is added to the NAFTA agenda, it will probably be as a result of the failure to ratify the agreement quickly, coupled with a lingering recession in California and other immigrant-receiving states. Alternatively, Mexico could put migration back on the table, perhaps in response to US labor and environmental side agreements, since President Salinas is under pressure to do something to protect Mexican workers in the United States. If the NAFTA ratification timetable slips, then issues such as immigration that have thus far avoided the limelight are more likely to be considered in the ratification debate.

Delay and continued recession increase the chances that California and other immigrant-receiving areas might link their support for NAFTA to requests for Migration Adjustment Assistance (MAA). Hard-hit state and local governments are blaming the failure of federal immigration policies for some of their burgeoning education, health, and public safety costs. In the case of California, it is estimated that 10 percent of the state's $51 billion budget is devoted to providing these services for recent arrivals. The debate over the impact of immigrants on tax revenues and public service costs resonates with many Americans, and polls indicate that most Americans would like to see immigration levels reduced. For example, a June 1993 *New York Times*/CBS News poll found that 61 percent of those surveyed think that the level of immigration should be reduced, while only 7 percent think that the number of immigrants should be increased (*The New York Times*, 27 June 1993, 1).

As the source of one-third of the nation's legal immigrants and half of the illegal settlers, Mexico figures prominently in this backlash against immigration. NAFTA can eventually reduce incentives to migrate, thus diminishing the numbers that worry many Americans, but few are aware that growth-stimulating policies such as NAFTA initially increase migration. If complaining state and local governments do not get at least partial federal reimbursement for the costs they are incurring for integrating newcomers, they may look to NAFTA as a vehicle to extract such reimbursement.

It is not clear just how much federal reimbursement is justified. The most recent review of the fiscal impacts of immigration concluded that "current federal policy creates negative spillover effects or externalities for state and local governments, and because these externalities are not fully internalized, the immigration door is open wider than it otherwise would be" (Rothman and Espenshade 1992, 410), largely because unskilled immigrants pay primarily Social Security taxes to the federal government but use education, health, and criminal justice services, which are provided by state and local governments. Since NAFTA involves the major source country of immigrants and because associated state and local government costs are more than $10 billion in just one state, MAA may yet figure prominently in the NAFTA debate.

If migration makes its way onto the NAFTA negotiating table, the federal government should have a plan to respond. Many of the equity, efficiency, and political efficacy arguments for Trade Adjustment Assistance (TAA) could also be marshaled in support of federal Migration Adjustment Assistance (MAA). The federal government is responsible for regulating immigration into the United States, and immigrants have a well-known tendency to cluster in a few states and cities. The absence of federal assistance to absorb immigrants could provoke a restrictionist backlash in the areas where they cluster. In the absence of adequate general programs to assist immigrants and their dependents, a categorical MAA program of federal assistance to state and local governments may be the second-best solution (Aho and Bayard 1984, 154–62).

Finally, Mexico could put migration on the NAFTA negotiating table. Mexico originally wanted to broach the issue but was dissuaded by US negotiators. However, the issue lurks just beneath the surface. The Mexican government's submission to the current GATT round of negotiations included the assertion that "the expansion of the service exports of developing countries . . . depends on the liberalization of cross-border movement of personnel, covering unskilled, semi-skilled, and skilled labor" (quoted in Donahue 1991). Mexican President Salinas in November 1990 acknowledged that migration would not be part of the NAFTA negotiations, but then went on to note that "this flow of people is a matter of reality, one which we will have to sit down sooner or later to talk about." After asserting that 90 percent of the Mexican immigrants who enter the United States eventually return to Mexico, Salinas called for the eventual "free mobility of labor," adding that, "if it is understood that we are talking about migration and not immigration, then that difference can have an impact on the talks that we may eventually have" (*San Diego Union*, 14 November 1990, A4).

Salinas echoed a number of Mexican and American scholars when he asserted that Mexican workers already have fairly free access to the US labor market and that these workers would not migrate if they were not needed by the US employers who offer them jobs. His complaint is that this migration "is happening under very harsh circumstances because the abuses of Mexican migrant workers on both sides of the border are unacceptable. . . . I think that we should organize [the migrant flow] formally in order to avoid the abuses." (*San Diego Union*, 14 November 1990, A4).

It is not clear what the outcome of bilateral migration negotiations would be. There have been proposals to expand the legal immigration quota for Mexico or to combine the Mexican and Canadian quotas into a single North American quota, which would effectively give Mexico more immigrant slots, but such proposals run counter to the post-1965 policy that moves away from national-origins favoritism. Mexico could request that unauthorized Mexican workers be converted into legal non-immigrant guestworkers. However, as the experience with the postwar Bracero program demonstrated, such programs very quickly can create as many problems as they solve, and opposition to temporary worker programs is one of the few common goals of anti-NAFTA unions, ethnic groups, and immigration control organizations.

If Migration Is Considered

If migration becomes important in NAFTA ratification, two facts should be borne in mind. First, legal and illegal Mexico-to-US migration is already significant, and NAFTA will add only incrementally to the flow. Second, NAFTA is likely to eventually reduce migration, so that its implementation should not be contingent upon creation of a better US immigration control system.

If migration takes center stage, it should be treated in a fashion similar to border environmental problems. These problems were serious before NAFTA, and they should be dealt with regardless of NAFTA. NAFTA provides the catalyst for long overdue action. Just as the environmental side agreement should provide a mechanism to clean up existing problem areas and to encourage the type and location of new facilities in areas where they will create fewer problems, so a migration agreement could lay the basis for Mexican actions to stem emigration and bilateral cooperation in immigration control. For example, the United States could encourage Mexico to enforce existing migration laws, such as the law that prohibits Mexicans from leaving the country except from official departure points. Once migration is on the table, it should also be possible to discuss policies that could encourage the movement of NAFTA-created jobs away from the border area to minimize stepping-stone migration.

Immigration from Mexico is a problem that predates NAFTA, and NAFTA will aggravate it only marginally and temporarily. Holding NAFTA hostage to new agreements on this problem will only delay its resolution.

9

Policy Options

Can NAFTA do indirectly what the Immigration Reform and Control Act of 1986 could not do directly—that is, reduce Mexico-to-US migration? The answer is a qualified yes. NAFTA is likely to accelerate economic growth, especially in Mexico. Since emigration is usually a last rather than a first resort, economic opportunity in Mexico should create new options that make it less necessary to "go north." However, this migration-dampening effect only follows a period of 5 to 10 years of more migration—the migration hump.

This migration hump should be considered a reasonable price for eventually reducing emigration pressures. It should involve no more than an additional 20,000 to 30,000 Mexican immigrants annually, or the equivalent of adding an extra year's immigration from Mexico over the agreement's first decade. Furthermore, NAFTA can be implemented in a manner that reduces the size and duration of the hump.

In order to develop policy options to deal with both the underlying migration issue as well as the migration hump, it must be acknowledged that Mexico accounts for one-third of US immigration and that a short-term increase in Mexico-to-US migration is probable under NAFTA. Immigration is likely to increase during the 1990s because of continuing US demand-pull for Mexican workers, higher supply-push pressures in rural Mexico, and networks that make it possible for Mexicans to migrate legally and illegally into the United States. Most analyses of NAFTA and migration emphasize that freer trade in corn, which will add to supply-push emigration pressures, is the primary reason to expect a migration hump. However, all three factors are important, and it is very difficult to prove that any one factor plays a disproportionate role in determining migration flows.

Implement NAFTA, Renew Control Efforts, and Integrate Newcomers

With three factors determining migration flows, there is a need for multiple policy responses. *The most important US policy response is to implement NAFTA as scheduled.* The US demand-pull of jobs plays an important role in determining how many Mexicans move to the United States, and delaying NAFTA simply preserves in the United States some industries and jobs that depend on Mexican immigrant workers. The United States should not hope and need not fear that such industries and jobs will disappear as a result of NAFTA: even in agriculture, climatic factors promise to keep most of North America's fruit and vegetable jobs in the United States.

Second, the United States could cooperate with Mexico to reduce supply-push emigration there. Mexico is trying to design land and farm policies that increase economic efficiency and improve equity. The United States has experience with the effects of efficiency-increasing farm policies on rural depopulation, since the United States had a net transfer of over 1 million farmers and their families annually to urban areas between 1945 and 1965; the "great migration" that accompanied changes in US agriculture has been acknowledged as a source of urban problems.

Mexico has already made a number of agricultural policy changes that have migration consequences. Input subsidies have been reduced, restrictions on foreign and corporate investment in agriculture have been relaxed, and *ejido* farmers are becoming landowners. A major remaining issue is how to reduce high price guarantees for the corn and beans many small farmers grow. If Mexico "decouples" production from support—that is, if farmers receive a check whether they grow the crop or not—then a rural economy already adapted to external remittances may gain another external lifeline. Such a decoupling is likely to increase emigration pressures: with fewer farm jobs, landless workers may have to migrate, and small farmers may elect to get both remittances and a farm support check. Mexico should be willing to reform its rural policies in ways that do not aggravate emigration, and the United States should be ready to help Mexico achieve that goal.

There are also several options that could help to shrink and manage the migration networks that link Mexico and the United States. The United States should secure Mexico's cooperation in dealing with illegal border crossings. Mexico has already cooperated with the United States to slow the movement of Central Americans en route to the United

States, but Mexico could do much more to prevent Mexicans and other aliens from massing at the US border, waiting to cross until their numbers are sufficient to overwhelm Border Patrol agents. There is a limited precedent for such cooperation: in the Tijuana–San Diego area, Mexican police have on several occasions prevented groups of Mexicans from rushing through the port-of-entry and then attempting to run into the United States in the median strip of a freeway, on the grounds that they endangered themselves in freeway traffic. Aliens apprehended in the United States are simply bused to the Mexican border and released. If the United States and Mexico really wanted to deter illegal entries, they should cooperate to return those apprehended to their areas of origin— it is far more costly to attempt another illegal entry from a village 1,000 miles from the border than from a border city.

The United States could also do more unilaterally to control immigration. A number of perennial debates may have to be resolved before US immigration control efforts can become more effective, including whether the United States can have a universal work authorization document (or 50 state documents) without threatening civil liberties. The Immigration and Naturalization Service may have to review its enforcement strategies, and a new system of penalties may have to be explored in order to convince US employers that knowingly hiring an illegal alien is a serious offense.

Immigration cooperation and control will help to reduce the migration hump, but the United States should also anticipate and deal with what promises to be more rather than less migration during the 1990s. Two federal initiatives stand out: Migration Adjustment Assistance (MAA) and programs to promote the integration of recent Mexican immigrants.

US immigrants are bimodal in the sense that they tend to be either better educated than the average US resident or less educated. Mexican immigrants tend to be in the lesser-educated tier; the average Mexican immigrant has only a primary school education. During the 1980s, economic growth obscured the fact that the Social Security taxes paid by unskilled immigrant workers flow to the federal government, while the costs attributed to them tend to be borne by state and local governments. This federal-state cost shifting existed long before NAFTA. However, just as with border environmental problems, NAFTA may provide the catalyst to deal with a dilemma that preceded the agreement.

The federal government could head off potential opposition to NAFTA as well as a backlash against immigrants with Migration Adjustment Assistance (MAA) programs to aid state and local governments receiving large numbers of immigrants. MAA does not have to become a usual part of trade agreements in the way that Trade Adjustment Assistance (TAA) programs are geared to workers displaced by increased imports. State and local governments deserve MAA whether the immigrants they receive entered the United States illegally as a result of a trade agreement, as a result of the federal government's immigration control failures, or because federal policies admit needy legal immigrants or act to legalize illegal aliens. MAA programs should be general programs that help local areas affected by federal policies, not trade-specific migration policies that would require elaborate accounting procedures to determine why the migrant came in order to establish local government eligibility for local reimbursement.

Cooperation to control immigration and federal assistance for state and local governments can reduce the number of immigrants and the backlash against them, but these steps are unlikely to eliminate illegal immigration from Mexico. The United States also needs to develop an integration strategy for the Mexicans expected to arrive in the 1990s.

Past integration policies were based on a growing economy. Unskilled European immigrants who arrived at the beginning of the 20th century most often found jobs in urban areas, and under union pressures, the immigrants and American workers shared in the country's growth. Today's economy seems to be evolving in ways that make it difficult for poorly educated workers to enjoy rising real wages. Since Mexican immigrants fit this profile, those that arrive during the 1990s might have a difficult time successfully integrating into the American economy.

Just as NAFTA should not be held hostage to more fundamental immigration control questions, neither is it an excuse to rethink all the programs through which the United States tries to assist disadvantaged workers and their children. But NAFTA promises to affect primarily immigration from rural Mexico to rural America, so the agreement does provide a reason to reexamine the first federal programs with which most Mexican immigrants come in contact: those that assist migrant and seasonal farm workers (MSFWs) and their families. The federal government spends almost as much money on these programs—over $600 million annually—as it does on TAA (table 10).

Federal programs for disadvantaged MSFWs were developed in the 1960s under a rationale similar to other programs for the needy: that is, those not helped by a growing economy needed intensive services. This model of intensive services for individuals in targeted groups is relatively expensive and often has high administrative costs, as program operators must determine whether a particular person is eligible for assistance.

Instead of more federal funding for these programs, which since the 1960s have shifted from serving disadvantaged US citizens to serving Mexican immigrants, it may be time to rethink what services this new clientele needs to succeed in the United States. The single most important obstacle to upward economic mobility for rural Mexican immigrants is lack of English language skills. Even though the opportunity to learn English is often identified as a significant factor in lowering immigrant

Table 10   US migrant and seasonal farm worker programs, fiscal 1992 and 1988[a]

Program	Department	Services	Funding in fiscal 1992 (millions of dollars)	Funding in fiscal 1988 (millions of dollars)	Percentage change
Migrant Education	Education	Funds state educational agencies (SEAs) to serve the children of migrants who are age 3 to 21	308.3	269.0	14.6
Migrant Health	HHS	Funds clinics that provide primary health care for MSFWs and their dependents	57.7	43.5	32.6
Job Training Partnership Act 402	Labor	Employment and training services for MSFWs and their dependents	77.6	65.6	18.3
Migrant Head Start	HHS	Early childhood program for migrant children age 0 to 5	85.9	40.5	112.1
Total "big four" programs			529.5	418.6	26.5
High-School Equivalency	Education	Funds colleges and universities to assist migrants and their dependents to get a high school diploma or equivalent	8.3	7.3	13.7
College Assistance Migrant Program	Education	Funds colleges and universities to help migrants and their dependents ease their transition into college	2.3	1.3	76.9
Migrant Even Start	Education	Funds programs to coordinate child and adult education for migrants	2.1		
Migrant vocational rehabilitation	Education	Funds programs for handicapped migrants	1.0	1.1	−9.1
Migrant Women, Infants, and Children	USDA	Provides food and nutrition counseling to poor women and children	17.5	13.0	34.6

Table 10 US migrant and seasonal farm worker programs, fiscal 1992 and 1988 (Continued)[a]

Program	Department	Services	Funding in fiscal 1992 (millions of dollars)	Funding in fiscal 1988 (millions of dollars)	Percentage change
Migrant legal services	Legal Services Corp.	Provides legal services to MSFWs	10.8	9.4	14.9
Section 516 MSFW housing grants	USDA	Makes grants to nonprofit organizations for farm worker housing	11.0	11.2	−1.8
Section 514 MSFW housing loans	USDA	Makes loans to farmers and nonprofits for farm worker housing	16.3	11.4	42.9
Community services block grants	HHS	Funds block grants reserved for farm workers	3.0	3.0	0.0
Subtotal			72.3	57.7	25.3
Total			601.8	476.3	26.3

a. These programs serve only MSFWs or reserve a portion of a larger program for them. MSFWs also participate in other programs for which they qualify, including food stamps, AFDC, literacy programs, homeless programs, bilingual and immigrant education, and low-income home energy assistance programs.

Source: AFOP Washington Newsline, November/December 1991, p. 3 and June 1988, p. 3, supplemented by interviews with agency officials.

earnings, programs that were begun for US citizens have been slow to recognize the needs of their immigrant recipients. Federal MSFW programs might blaze a trail for immigrant integration in the 1990s by switching their emphasis from intensive services for a few individuals to language assistance for large groups.

The NAFTA Promise

NAFTA marks a milestone in US-Mexican relations. For the United States, it promises an eventual solution to the vexing problem of illegal immigration. For Mexico, NAFTA promises the economic growth and jobs needed so that its citizens do not have to migrate illegally to improve their standard of living. Free trade can be implemented in many ways: the United States needs to ensure that the agreement solves the problem of illegal immigration as quickly as possible.

NAFTA can eventually eliminate the migration that has so often been a sore point in US-Mexican relations. To deal with this migration, the United States and Mexico must avoid blaming each other for the problem and work separately and cooperatively on the three elements that encourage this migration: the demand-pull of US jobs, the supply-push of Mexican poverty, and the networks that link Mexico and the United States. Mexico and the United States can and should address these factors while implementing NAFTA as planned so that free trade and stay-at-home development can go hand-in-hand in North America.

References

Abadan-Unat, Nermin, Rusan Keles, Rinus Penninx, Herman van Renselaar, Leo van Vlezen, and Leyla Yenisey. 1976. *Migration and Development: A Study of the Effects of International Labor Migration on Bogaziliyan District*. Ankara: Ajams-Turk Press.

Abowd, John M., and Richard B. Freeman, eds. 1991. *Immigration, Trade and the Labor Market*. Chicago: University of Chicago Press for the National Bureau of Economic Research.

Acevedo, Dolores., and Thomas Espenshade. 1992. "Implications of a NAFTA for Mexican Migration into the United States." *Population and Development Review* 18, 4 (December): 729–44.

Adler, Stephen. 1981. *A Turkish Conundrum: Emigration, Politics, and Development, 1961–1980*. Geneva: International Labor Organization.

Aho, C. Michael, and Thomas Bayard. 1984. "Costs and Benefits of Trade Adjustment Assistance." In Robert Baldwin and Anne Krueger, eds., *The Structure and Evolution of Recent US Trade Policy*. Chicago: University of Chicago Press.

Alarcon, Rafael. 1992. "*Norteizacion*: Self-Perpetuating Migration from a Mexican Town." In Jorge Bustamante, Clark Reynolds, and Raul Hinojosa-Ojeda, eds., *U.S. Mexican Relations: Labor Market Interdependence*. Stanford, CA: Stanford University Press.

Alba, Francisco. 1978. "Mexico's International Migration as a Manifestation of Development Pattern." *International Migration Review* 12 (Winter): 502–13.

Alba, Francisco. 1992. "Migrant Labor Supply and Demand in Mexico and the United States: A Global Perspective." In Jorge Bustamante, Clark Reynolds, and Raul Hinojosa-Ojeda, eds., *U.S. Mexican Relations: Labor Market Interdependence*. Stanford, CA: Stanford University Press.

Alvarado, Andy, Herbert Mason, Gary Riley, and John Hagen. 1992. "The Raisin Industry in California." In appendix II of the Report of the Commission on Agricultural Workers. Washington: US Government Printing Office.

Appleyard, Reginald. 1989. "Migration and Development: Myths and Reality." *International Migration Review* 23, 3 (Fall): 486–99.

Ascencio, Fernando. 1993. *Bringing It Back Home: Remittances to Mexico from Migrant Workers in the United States*. La Jolla, CA: University of California–San Diego, Center for U.S.-Mexican Studies.

Auditor General of California. 1992. "A Fiscal Impact Analysis of Undocumented Immigrants Residing in San Diego County." Sacramento: Auditor General's Office.

Banamex. 1990. *Review of the Mexican Economy.* Mexico City: Banamex (September).

Barkema, Alan. 1992. "The North American Free Trade Agreement: What Is at Stake for U.S. Agriculture." *Economic Review of the Federal Reserve Bank of Kansas City* 77, 3 (Third Quarter): 5–20.

Bean, Frank, Jurgen Schmandt, and Sidney Weintraub, eds. 1989. *Mexican and Central American Population and U.S. Immigration Policy.* Austin: Center for Mexican American Studies, University of Texas.

Bean, Frank, Barry Edmonston, and Jeffrey Passel, eds. 1990. *Undocumented Migration to the United States: IRCA and the Experience of the 1980s.* Washington: The Urban Institute Press.

Böhning, W. R. 1972. *The Migration of Workers in the United Kingdom and the European Community.* Oxford: Oxford University Press for the Institute of Race Relations.

Böhning, W. R. 1984. *Studies in International Labor Migration.* London: Macmillan.

Böhning, W. R., and M. Schloeter-Paredes. 1993. *Economic Haven or Political Refugees: Can Aid Reduce the Need for Migration?* Proceedings of a May 1992 ILO-UNHCR Conference. Geneva: International Labor Organization.

Borjas, George J. 1990. *Friends or Strangers: The Impact of Immigrants on the U.S. Economy.* New York: Basic Books.

Brannon, Jeffrey T., and G. William Lucker. 1988. "The Impact of Mexico's Economic Crisis on the Demographic Composition of the Maquiladora Labor Force." Report prepared for the US Department of Labor, and article in the *Journal of Borderlands Studies* 4, 1 (Spring 1989): 39–70.

Briggs, Vernon. 1984. *Immigration Policy and the American Labor Force.* Baltimore: Johns Hopkins University Press.

Briggs, Vernon, Jr. 1992. *Mass Immigration and the National Interest.* Armonk, NY: M. E. Sharpe.

Brown, G. K. 1984. "Fruit and Vegetable Mechanization." In Philip Martin, ed., *Migrant Labor in Agriculture: An International Comparison.* Berkeley, CA: Giannini Foundation.

Bustamante, Jorge, Clark Reynolds, and Raul Hinojosa-Ojeda, eds. 1992. *U.S. Mexican Relations: Labor Market Interdependence.* Stanford, CA: Stanford University Press.

Callovi, G. 1990. "Regulating Immigration in the European Community." Paper presented to the CES Europeanists Conference in Washington, DC, 23–25, March 1990.

Calva, Jose Luis. 1992. *Probables Efectos de un Tratado de Libre Comercio en el Campo Mexico.* Mexico City: Fontamara.

Cardenas, Gil. 1975. "U.S. Immigration Policy toward Mexico: An Historical Perspective." *Chicano Law Review* 2.

Cargill, B. F. and G. E. Rossmiller, eds. 1970. *Fruit and Vegetable Harvest Mechanization.* East Lansing, MI: Rural Manpower Center.

Coale, Ansley. 1978. "Population Growth and Economic Development: The Case of Mexico." *Foreign Affairs* 56, 2 (January): 415–29.

Comisión Economica para América Latina y el Caribe (CEPAL). 1989. "Magnitude de pobreza en America Latina en los anos ochenta." LC/L533. Santiago: CEPAL.

Commission on Agricultural Workers. 1992. "Final Report." Washington: Government Printing Office.

Cook, Roberta, Carlos Benito, James Matson, David Runsten, Kenneth Shwedel, and Timothy Taylor. 1991. "Fruits and Vegetable Issues" *NAFTA: Effects on Agriculture,* vol. 4. Park Ridge, IL: American Farm Bureau Foundation.

Congressional Research Service. 1980. "Temporary Worker Programs: Background and Issues." Prepared for the Senate Committee on the Judiciary (February).

Cornelius, Wayne. 1990. *Labor Migration to the U.S.: Development Outcomes and Alternatives in Mexican Sending Communities.* La Jolla, CA: Center for U.S.-Mexican Studies, University of California–San Diego (March).

Cornelius, Wayne. 1991. "Impacts of NAFTA on Mexican Labor Migration." Manuscript (4 May).

Cornelius, Wayne. 1992a. "The Politics and Economics of Reforming the Ejido Sector in Mexico: An Overview and Research Agenda." *LASA Forum* 23, 3: 3–10.

Cornelius, Wayne. 1992b. "From Sojourners to Settlers: The Changing Profile of Mexican Immigration to the United States." In Jorge Bustamante, Clark Reynolds, and Raul Hinojosa-Ojeda, eds., *U.S. Mexican Relations: Labor Market Interdependence*. Stanford, CA: Stanford University Press.

Council of Economic Advisers. 1986. "The Economic Effects of Immigration." *Economic Report of the President*. Washington: Council of Economic Advisers.

Craig, Richard B. 1971. *The Bracero Program: Interest Groups and Foreign Policy*. Austin: University of Texas Press.

Cross, Harry, and James Sandos. 1981. *Across the Border: Rural Development in Mexican and Recent Migration to the United States*. Berkeley, CA: Institute of Governmental Studies, University of California.

Dávila, Alberto, and Rogelio Saenz. 1990. "The Effect of Maquiladora Employment on the Monthly Flow of Mexican Undocumented Immigration to the U.S., 1978–1982." *International Migration Review* 24, 1: 96–107.

Donahue, Thomas R. 1991. Testimony before US Senate Committee on Finance (6 February).

Espenshade, Thomas. 1991. "Responsiveness of the Mexico-U.S. Flow of Undocumented Migrants to Relative Improvements in the Mexican Economy." Manuscript.

Faux, Jeff, and Thea Lee. 1992. *The Effect of George Bush's NAFTA on American Workers: Ladder Up or Ladder Down?* Washington: Economic Policy Institute.

Fix, Michael. 1991. *The Paper Curtain: Employer Sanctions, Implementation, Impact, and Reform*. Washington: Urban Institute Press.

Fix, Michael, and Paul Hill. 1990. *Enforcing Employer Sanctions: Challenges and Strategies*. Washington: Urban Institute Press.

Fogel, Walt. 1977. "Illegal Alien Workers in the United States." *Industrial and Labor Relations Review* 16.

Fuller, Varden. 1942. "The Supply of Agricultural Labor as a Factor in the Evolution of Farm Organization in California." In *Violations of Free Speech and the Rights of Labor Education and Labor Committee*, report of the LaFollette Committee. Washington: Senate Education and Labor Committee.

Garcia y Griego, Manuel. 1981. *The Importation of Mexican Contract Laborers to the U.S., 1941–1964*. Program in U.S.-Mexican Studies, UCSD Working Paper 11. La Jolla, CA: University of California–San Diego, Center for U.S.-Mexican Studies.

Garcia y Griego, Manuel. 1989. "The Mexican Labor Supply, 1990–2010." In Wayne Cornelius and Jorge A. Bustamante, eds., *Mexican Migration to the United States: Origins, Consequences and Policy Options*. La Jolla, CA: University of California–San Diego, Center for U.S.-Mexican Studies.

Grayson, George. 1993. *The North American Free Trade Agreement*. New York: Foreign Policy Association.

Gregory, Peter. 1991. "The Determinants of International Migration and Policy Options for Influencing the Size of Population Flows." In Sergio Díaz-Briquets and Sidney Weintraub, eds., *Determinants of Emigration from Mexico, Central America, and the Caribbean* vol 1. Boulder, CO: Westview Press.

Grindle, Merilee. 1988. *Searching for Rural Development*. Ithaca, NY: Cornell University Press.

Grunwald, Joseph, and Kenneth Flamm. 1985. *The Global Factory: Foreign Assembly in International Trade*. Washington: The Brookings Institution.

Hayes-Bautista, David, Werner Schink, and Jorge Chapa. 1992. "The Young Latino Population in an Aging American Society: Policy Issues Evoked by the Emergence of an Age-

Race Stratified Society." In Jorge Bustamante, Clark Reynolds, and Raul Hinojosa-Ojeda, eds., *U.S. Mexican Relations: Labor Market Interdependence*. Stanford, CA: Stanford University Press.

Hiemenz, U., and K. W. Schatz. 1979. *Trade in Place of Migration: An Employment-Oriented Study with Special References to the Federal Republic of the Federal Republic of Germany, Spain and Turkey*. Geneva: International Labor Office.

Hightower, James. 1978. *Hard Tomatoes, Hard Times*. Cambridge, MA: Schenkman Publishing Company.

Hinojosa-Ojeda, Raul, and Sherman Robinson. 1991a. "Alternative Scenarios of U.S.-Mexico Integration: A Computable General Equilibrium Approach." Working Paper No. 609. Berkeley, CA: Department of Agricultural and Resource Economics, University of California.

Hinojosa-Ojeda, Raul, and Sherman Robinson. 1991b. "Labor Issues in a North American Free Trade Area." In Nora Lustig, Barry Bosworth, and Robert Lawrence, eds., *North American Free Trade: Assessing the Impact*. Washington: The Brookings Institution.

Hinojosa-Ojeda, Raul, Sherman Robinson, and Geotz Wolff. 1991. "The Impact of a North American Free Trade Agreement on California: A Summary of Key Research Findings." Lewis Center for Regional Policy Studies Working Paper No. 3 (September). Los Angeles: University of California.

Hinojosa-Ojeda, Raul, and Robert McCleery. 1992. "U.S.-Mexico Interdependence, Social Pacts and Policy Perspectives: A Computable General Equilibrium Approach." In Jorge Bustamante, Clark Reynolds, and Raul Hinojosa-Ojeda, eds., *U.S. Mexican Relations: Labor Market Interdependence*. Stanford, CA: Stanford University Press.

Hollifield, James. 1992. *Immigrants, Markets, and States: the Political Economy of Immigration in Postwar Europe and the U.S*. Cambridge: Harvard University Press.

Hönekopp, Elmar. 1992. "Auswirkungen eines EG-Beitritts der Turkei auf Demographie und Arbeitsmarkt in der Eg und in Deutschland." Manuscript (February).

Huerta, Mario M. Carillo. 1990a. *The Impact of Maquiladoras on Migration in Mexico*. Working Paper 51 (July). Washington: US Commission for the Study of International Migration and Cooperative Economic Development.

Huerta, Mario M. Carillo. 1990b. *Maquiladoras y Migracion en Mexico*. Puebla: Asesoria y Consultoria Economica.

Hufbauer, Gary, and Jeffrey Schott. 1992. *North American Free Trade: Issues and Recommendations*. Washington: Institute for International Economics.

Hufbauer, Gary, and Jeffrey Schott. 1993. *NAFTA: An Assessment*. Washington: Institute for International Economics.

Johnson, William B. 1987. *Workforce 2000: Work and Workers for the 21st Century*. Report to the US Department of Labor. Indianapolis: Hudson Institute.

Kindleberger, Charles P. 1967. *Europe's Postwar Growth: The Role of Labor Supply*. Cambridge, MA: Harvard University Press.

Krauss, M. B. 1976. "The Economics of the 'Guest Worker' Problem: A Neo-Heckscher-Ohlin Approach." *Scandinavian Journal of Economics* 78: 470–76.

Layard, Richard, Oliver Blanchard, Rudiger Dornbusch, and Paul Krugman. 1992. *East West Migration: The Alternatives*. Cambridge, MA: MIT Press.

Levy, Santiago, and Sweder van Wijnbergen. 1992. "Mexico and the Free Trade Agreement between Mexico and the United States." *The World Bank Economic Review* 4, 3: 481–502.

London, Joan, and Henry Anderson. 1970. *So Shall Ye Reap*. New York: Thomas Crowell.

Los Angeles County. 1992. "Impact of Undocumented Persons and Other Immigrants on Costs, Revenues and Services in Los Angeles County" (6 November).

Lusting, Nora. 1992. *Mexico: The Remaking of an Economy*. Washington: Brookings Institution.

Majka, Linda, and Theo Majka. 1982. *Farmworkers, Agribusiness, and the State*. Philadelphia: Temple University Press.

Martin, Philip. 1980. *Guestworker Programs: Lessons from Europe*. Washington: Department of Labor, International Labor Affairs Bureau.

Martin, Philip. 1983. *Labor Displacement and Public Policy.* Lexington, MA: Lexington Books.

Martin, Philip. 1990."The Outlook for Agricultural Labor in the 1990s." *UC Davis Law Review* 23, 3 (Spring): 499–523.

Martin, Philip. 1991. *The Unfinished Story: Turkish Labor Migration to Western Europe.* Geneva: International Labor Organization.

Martin, Philip. 1993. "Germany: Reluctant Land of Immigration." In Wayne Cornelius, James Hollifield, and Philip L. Martin, eds., *Controlling Immigration: A Global Perspective.* La Jolla, CA: NSF Project Report (forthcoming).

Martin, Philip. 1994. "Collective Bargaining in Agriculture." In Paula Voos, ed., *Contemporary Collective Bargaining in the Private Sector.* Madison, WI: Industrial Relations Research Association. Forthcoming.

Martin, Philip, Elmar Hönekopp, and Hans Ulmann. 1990. "Europe 1992: Effects on Labor Migration." *International Migration Review* 24, 91 (Fall): 591–603.

Martin, Philip, and David Martin. 1993. *The Endless Quest: Helping America's Farmworkers.* Boulder, CO: Westview Press.

Martin, Philip, and Alan Olmsted. 1985. "The Agricultural Mechanization Controversy." *Science* 227, 4687 (8 February): 601–06.

Massey, Douglas S. 1988. "Economic Development and International Migration in Comparative Perspective." *Population and Development Review* 14, 3 (September): 383–413.

Massey, Douglas S. 1991. "Economic Development and International Migration in Comparative Perspective." In Sergio Diaz-Briquets and Sidney Weintraub, eds., *Determinants of Emigration From Mexico, Central America, and the Caribbean* 1. Boulder: Westview Press.

Massey, Douglas, Rafael Alarcon, Jorge Durand, and Humberto Gonzales. 1987. *Return to Aztlan: The Social Process of International Migration from Western Mexico.* Berkeley, CA: University of California Press.

Massey, Douglas, Katherine Donato, and Zai Lang. 1990. "Effects of the Immigration Reform and Control Act of 1986: Preliminary Data from Mexico." In Frank Bean, Barry Edmonston, and Jeffrey Passel, eds., *Undocumented Migration to the United States: IRCA and the Experience of the 1980s.* Washington: The Urban Institute Press.

Massey, D., and J. Durand. 1992. "Mexican Migration to the United States." *Latin American Research Review* (Spring): 3–42.

Miller, Mark, and Philip Martin. 1982. *Administering Foreign Worker Programs.* Lexington, MA: Lexington Books.

Mines, Richard. 1982. *The Evolution of Mexican Migration to the U.S.: A Case Study.* Berkeley, CA: Giannini Foundation.

Mines, Richard, Susan Gabbard, and Beatriz Boccalandro. 1991. *Findings from the NAWS 1990.* Research Report No. 1. Washington: US Department of Labor, Office of Assistant Secretary for Policy.

Mines, Richard, Susan Gabbard, and Ruth Samardick. 1993. *US Farmworkers in the Post-IRCA Period.* Research Report No. 4. Washington: US Department of Labor, Office of the Assistant Secretary for Policy.

Muller, Thomas, and Thomas Espenshade. 1985. *The Fourth Wave: California's Newest Immigrants.* Washington: The Urban Institute Press.

Mundell, R. A. 1957. "International Trade and Factor Mobility." *American Economic Review* 47: 321–35.

Nagel, John. 1978. *Mexico's Population Policy Turnaround.* Washington: Population Reference Bureau.

National Council on Employment Policy. 1976. *Illegal Aliens: An Assessment of the Issues: A Policy Statement and Conference Report with Background Papers.* Washington: NCEP.

North, David, and Marion Houstoun. 1976. "The Characteristics and Role of Illegal Aliens in the U.S. Labor Market: An Exploratory Study." Washington: New Transcentury.

Oliveira, Victor, and Jane Cox. 1989. *The Agricultural Work Force of 1987: A Statistical Profile.* USDA-ERS-AER 609. Washington: US Department of Agriculture, Economic Research Service.

Paine, Suzanne. 1974. *Exporting Workers: The Turkish Case.* Cambridge (UK): Cambridge University Press.

Papademetriou, Demetrios, and Philip Martin, eds. 1991. *The Unsettled Relationship: Labor Migration and Economic Development.* Westport, CT: Greenwood Press.

Penninx, Rinus. 1982. "A Critical Review of Theory and Practice: The Case of Turkey." *International Migration Review* 16: 781–818.

Penninx, R., and P. Muus. 1989. "No Limits for Migration After 1992? The Lessons of the Past and a Reconnaissance of the Future." *International Migration Review* 28, 3 (September): 373.

Piore, Michael J. 1979. *Birds of Passage: Migrant Labor and Industrial Societies.* Cambridge (UK) and New York: Cambridge University Press.

Plummer, Charles. 1992. *US Tomato Statistics: 1960–90.* US Department of Agriculture, Economic Research Service, Statistical Bulletin No. 841. Washington: USDA.

Portes, Alejandro, and John Walton. 1981. *Labor, Class, and the International System.* New York: Academic Press.

President's Commission on Migratory Labor. 1951. *Migratory Labor in American Agriculture.* Washington: US Government Printing Office.

Reynolds, Clark. 1992. "Will a Free Trade Agreement Lead to Wage Convergence? Implications for Mexico and the United States." In Jorge Bustamante, Clark Reynolds, and Raul Hinojosa-Ojeda, eds., *U.S. Mexican Relations: Labor Market Interdependence.* Stanford, CA: Stanford University Press.

Robinson, Sherman, Mary E. Burfisher, Raul Hinojosa-Ojeda, and Karen E. Thierfelder. 1991. "Agricultural Policies and Migration in a U.S.-Mexico Free Trade Area: A Computable General Equilibrium Analysis." Working Paper No. 617. Berkeley, CA: Department of Agricultural and Resource Economics, University of California, Berkeley.

Rothman, Erik, and Thomas Espenshade. 1992. "Fiscal Impacts of Immigration to the United States." *Population Index* 58, 3 (Fall): 381–415.

Runsten, David. 1992. "Statement to the CAW." Printed in appendix II of the Final Report of the Commission on Agricultural Workers (November). Washington: CAW.

Salinas, Carlos. 1987. "The Maquiladoras of Mexico: An Effort to Understand the Controversy." *Southwest Journal of Business and Economics* 5, 1 (Fall).

Sanderson, Steven, ed. 1985. *The Americas in the New International Division of Labor.* New York: Holmes and Meier.

Schoepfle, Gregory, and Jorge Perez-Lopez. 1989. "Export Assembly Operations in Mexico and the Caribbean." *Journal of Inter-American Studies* 31, 4 (Winter).

Seligson, Mitchell, and Edward Williams. 1981. *Maquiladoras and Migration: A Study of Workers in the Mexican–United States Border Industrialization Program.* Austin: University of Texas, Mexico–United States Border Research Program.

Shimada, Huaro. 1993. "Foreign Workers in Japan." Manuscript.

Simon, Julian. 1981. *The Ultimate Resource.* Princeton, NJ: Princeton University Press.

Simcox, David. 1991. "Immigration and Free Trade with Mexico: Protecting American Workers Against Double Jeopardy." *Backgrounder No. 4-91* (December). Washington: Center for Immigration Studies.

Sklair, Leslie. 1989. *Assembling for Development: The Maquila Industry in Mexico and the United States.* Boston and London: Unwin Hyman.

Stahl, Charles W. 1982. "Labor Emigration and Economic Development." *International Migration Review* 16, 4: 869–99.

Stark, Oded. 1991. *The Migration of Labor.* Cambridge: Basil Blackwell.

Stoddard, Ellwyn. 1987. *Maquila: Assembly Plants in Northern Mexico.* El Paso: Texas Western Press.

Straubhaar, Thomas. 1987. "Freedom of Movement of Labour in a Common Market." *EFTA Bulletin* (April): 9–12.

Straubhaar, Thomas. 1988. *On the Economics of International Labor Migration.* Bern: Haupt.

Straubhaar, Thomas. 1992. "Allocational and Distributional Aspects of Future Immigration to Western Europe." *International Migration Review* 26, 2 (Summer): 462–83.

Taylor, J. E. 1987. "Undocumented Mexico-U.S. Migration and the Returns to Households in Rural Mexico." *American Journal of Agricultural Economics* 69: 626–38.

Taylor, J. E. 1992. "Remittances and inequality reconsidered: Direct, indirect, and intertemporal effects." *Journal of Policy Modeling* 14: 187–208.

Taylor, J. E., and T. J. Wyatt. 1992. "Migration, Assets, and Income Inequality." Working Paper 92–13. Davis, CA: University of California, Davis, Department of Agricultural Economics.

Teitelbaum, Michael. 1985. *Latin Migration North*. New York: Council on Foreign Relations.

Thomas, Brinley. 1973. *Migration and Economic Growth*. London: Cambridge University Press.

Thompson, Gary, and Philip Martin. 1989. *The Potential Effects of Labor Intensive Agriculture in Mexico on U.S.-Mexico Migration*. Working Paper 11 (December). Washington: Commission for the Study of Agricultural Workers.

Todaro, Michael. 1969. "A Model of Labor Migration and Urban Unemployment in Less Developed Countries." *American Economic Review* 59: 138–48.

US Agency for International Development. 1992. *Latin America and the Caribbean: Selected Economic and Social Data*. Washington: USAID.

US Commission for the Study of International Migration and Cooperative Economic Development. 1990. *Unauthorized Migration: An Economic Development Response*. Washington.

US Department of Agriculture. 1992. *Agriculture in a North American Free Trade Agreement*. Washington: USDA.

US Department of Labor, International Labor Affairs Bureau. 1989. *The Effects of Immigration on the US Economy*. Washington: ILAB.

US Department of Labor. 1991. *Findings From the NAWS: A Demographic and Employment Profile of Perishable Crop Farm Workers*. Washington: USDL.

US Department of Labor. 1993. *Educational Attainment of American Workers: Some New Data*. USDL 93-238 (July). Washington: USDL.

US Industrial Commission. 1901. *Reports, US Industrial Commission*, vol. 15, part 3. Washington: Government Printing Office.

Van Liemt, Gijsbert. 1988. *Bridging the Gap: Industrialising Countries and the Changing International Division of Labour*. Geneva: International Labor Organization.

Vernez, George, and Keven McCarthy. 1990. *Meeting the Economy's Labor Needs Through Immigration: Rationales and Challenges*. Rand Note N-3052-FF. Santa Monica: Rand Corporation.

Voos, Paula, ed. 1994. *Contemporary Collective Bargaining in the Private Sector*. Industrial Relations Research Association.

Wallerstein, Immanuel. 1974. *The Modern World System, Capitalist Agriculture and the Origins of the European World Economy in the Sixteenth Century*. New York: Academic Press.

Weintraub, Sidney. 1980. "North American Free Trade." *Challenge* (September–October): 48–51.

Weintraub, Sidney. 1984. *Free Trade between Mexico and the United States*. Washington: The Brookings Institution.

Weintraub, Sidney. 1990a. "The Maquiladora Industry in Mexico: Its Transitional Role." Working Paper 39 (June). Washington: Commission for the Study of International Migration and Cooperative Economic Development.

Weintraub, Sidney. 1990b. *A Marriage of Convenience: Relations between Mexico and the United States*. New York: Oxford University Press.

Weintraub, Sidney. 1992. "North American Free Trade and the European Situation Compared." *International Migration Review* 26, 2 (Summer): 506–24.

Williams, Edward. 1990. *The Unionization of the Maquiladora Industry: The Tamaulipan Case in National Context*. Report prepared for the US Department of Labor (July).

World Bank. 1992. *World Development Report 1992*. New York: Oxford University Press for the World Bank.

Yarbrough, Beth, and Robert Yarbrough. 1988. *The World Economy*. New York: Dryden Press.

Young, Linda Wilcox. "Internationalization of the Labor Process in Agriculture: A Case Study of Mexico's El Bajio." Unpublished Ph.D. thesis, University of California, Berkeley.

Yúnez-Naude, Antonio. 1991. "Towards a Free Trade Agreement Between Mexico and the USA: Effects on Mexican Primary, Non-Mineral Sectors." Unpublished paper (April). Mexico City: Centro de Estudios Económicos, El Colegio de México.

Yúnez-Naude, Antonio, and Ramón Blanno-Jasso. 1991. "Mexican Foreign Trade of Agricultural and Livestock Products: Tendencies and Impacts of Alternative Policies." In Sergio Diaz-Briquets and Sidney Weintraub, eds., *Regional and Sectoral Development in Mexico as Alternatives to Migration*. Boulder, CO: Westview.

Zabin, Carol, Michael Kearney, David Runsten, and Anna Garcia. 1993. *Mixtec Migrants in California Agriculture: A New Cycle of Rural Poverty*. Davis, CA: California Institute for Rural Studies.

Other Publications from the
Institute for International Economics

POLICY ANALYSES IN INTERNATIONAL ECONOMICS Series

1 **The Lending Policies of the International Monetary Fund**
John Williamson/*August 1982*
ISBN paper 0-88132-000-5   72 pp.

2 **"Reciprocity": A New Approach to World Trade Policy?**
William R. Cline/*September 1982*
ISBN paper 0-88132-001-3   41 pp.

3 **Trade Policy in the 1980s**
C. Fred Bergsten and William R. Cline/*November 1982*
(out of print)   ISBN paper 0-88132-002-1   84 pp.
Partially reproduced in the book *Trade Policy in the 1980s.*

4 **International Debt and the Stability of the World Economy**
William R. Cline/*September 1983*
ISBN paper 0-88132-010-2   134 pp.

5 **The Exchange Rate System, Second Edition**
John Williamson/*September 1983, rev. June 1985*
(out of print)   ISBN paper 0-88132-034-X   61 pp.

6 **Economic Sanctions in Support of Foreign Policy Goals**
Gary Clyde Hufbauer and Jeffrey J. Schott/*October 1983*
ISBN paper 0-88132-014-5   109 pp.

7 **A New SDR Allocation?**
John Williamson/*March 1984*
ISBN paper 0-88132-028-5   61 pp.

8 **An International Standard for Monetary Stabilization**
Ronald I. McKinnon/*March 1984*
ISBN paper 0-88132-018-8   108 pp.

9 **The Yen/Dollar Agreement: Liberalizing Japanese Capital Markets**
Jeffrey A. Frankel/*December 1984*
ISBN paper 0-88132-035-8   86 pp.

10 **Bank Lending to Developing Countries: The Policy Alternatives**
C. Fred Bergsten, William R. Cline, and John Williamson/*April 1985*
ISBN paper 0-88132-032-3   221 pp.

11 **Trading for Growth: The Next Round of Trade Negotiations**
Gary Clyde Hufbauer and Jeffrey J. Schott/*September 1985*
ISBN paper 0-88132-033-1   109 pp.

12 **Financial Intermediation Beyond the Debt Crisis**
Donald R. Lessard and John Williamson/*September 1985*
ISBN paper 0-88132-021-8   130 pp.

13 **The United States-Japan Economic Problem**
C. Fred Bergsten and William R. Cline/*October 1985, 2d ed. January 1987*
ISBN paper 0-88132-060-9   180 pp.

BOOKS

Completing the Uruguay Round: A Results-Oriented Approach to the GATT Trade Negotiations
Jeffrey J. Schott, editor/*September 1990*
ISBN paper 0-88132-130-3 256 pp.

Economic Sanctions Reconsidered (in two volumes)
  Economic Sanctions Reconsidered: History and Current Policy
  (also sold separately, see below)
  Economic Sanctions Reconsidered: Supplemental Case Histories
  Gary Clyde Hufbauer, Jeffrey J. Schott, and Kimberly Ann Elliott/*1985, 2d ed.*
  December 1990
ISBN cloth 0-88132-115-X 928 pp.
ISBN paper 0-88132-105-2 928 pp.

Economic Sanctions Reconsidered: History and Current Policy
Gary Clyde Hufbauer, Jeffrey J. Schott, and Kimberly Ann Elliott/*December 1990*
ISBN cloth 0-88132-136-2 288 pp.
ISBN paper 0-88132-140-0 288 pp.

Pacific Basin Developing Countries: Prospects for the Future
Marcus Noland/*January 1991*
ISBN cloth 0-88132-141-9 250 pp.
ISBN paper 0-88132-081-1 250 pp.

Currency Convertibility in Eastern Europe
John Williamson, editor/*October 1991*
ISBN cloth 0-88132-144-3 396 pp.
ISBN paper 0-88132-128-1 396 pp.

Foreign Direct Investment in the United States
Edward M. Graham and Paul R. Krugman/*1989, 2d ed. October 1991*
ISBN paper 0-88132-139-7 200 pp.

International Adjustment and Financing: The Lessons of 1985-1991
C. Fred Bergsten, editor/*January 1992*
ISBN paper 0-88132-112-5 336 pp.

North American Free Trade: Issues and Recommendations
Gary Clyde Hufbauer and Jeffrey J. Schott/*April 1992*
ISBN cloth 0-88132-145-1 392 pp.
ISBN paper 0-88132-120-6 392 pp.

American Trade Politics
I. M. Destler/*1986, rev. June 1992*
ISBN cloth 0-88132-164-8 400 pp.
ISBN paper 0-88132-188-5 400 pp.

Narrowing the U.S. Current Account Deficit
Allen J. Lenz/*June 1992*
ISBN cloth 0-88132-148-6 640 pp.
ISBN paper 0-88132-103-6 640 pp.

The Economics of Global Warming
William R. Cline/*June 1992*
ISBN cloth 0-88132-150-8 416 pp.
ISBN paper 0-88132-132-X 416 pp.

U.S. Taxation of International Income: Blueprint for Reform
Gary Clyde Hufbauer, assisted by Joanna M. van Rooij/*October 1992*

ISBN cloth 0-88132-178-8	304 pp.
ISBN paper 0-88132-134-6	304 pp.

Who's Bashing Whom? Trade Conflict in High-Technology Industries
Laura D'Andrea Tyson/*November 1992*

ISBN cloth 0-88132-151-6	352 pp.
ISBN paper 0-88132-106-0 .	352 pp.

Korea in the World Economy
Il Sakong/*January 1993*

ISBN cloth 0-88132-184-2	328 pp.
ISBN paper 0-88132-106-0	328 pp.

NAFTA: An Assessment
Gary Clyde Hufbauer and Jeffrey J. Schott/*February 1993, rev. ed. October 1993*

ISBN paper 0-88132-199-0	192 pp.

Pacific Dynamism and the International Economic System
C. Fred Bergsten and Marcus Noland, editors/*May 1993*

ISBN paper 0-88132-196-6	424 pp.

Economic Consequences of Soviet Disintegration
John Williamson, editor/*May 1993*

ISBN paper 0-88132-190-7	664 pp.

Reconcilable Differences? United States–Japan Economic Conflict
C. Fred Bergsten and Marcus Noland/*June 1993*

ISBN paper 0-88132-129-X	296 pp.

Does Foreign Exchange Intervention Work?
Kathryn M. Dominguez and Jeffrey A. Frankel/*September 1993*

ISBN 0-88132-104-4	192 pp.

Sizing Up U.S. Export Disincentives
J. David Richardson/*September 1993*

ISBN 0-88132-107-9	192 pp.

SPECIAL REPORTS

1 **Promoting World Recovery: A Statement on Global Economic Strategy by Twenty-six Economists from Fourteen Countries/** *December 1982*
   (out of print) ISBN paper 0-88132-013-7 45 pp.

2 **Prospects for Adjustment in Argentina, Brazil, and Mexico: Responding to the Debt Crisis**
   John Williamson, editor/*June 1983*
   (out of print) ISBN paper 0-88132-016-1 71 pp.

3 **Inflation and Indexation: Argentina, Brazil, and Israel**
   John Williamson, editor/*March 1985*
   ISBN paper 0-88132-037-4 191 pp.

4 **Global Economic Imbalances**
   C. Fred Bergsten, editor/*March 1986*

FORTHCOMING

For orders outside the US and Canada please contact:

Longman Group UK Ltd.
PO Box 88
Harlow, Essex CM 19 5SR
UK

Telephone Orders: 0279 623925
Fax: 0279 453450
Telex: 817484